Competitiveness and Private Sector Development

Women's Economic Empowerment in Selected MENA Countries

THE IMPACT OF LEGAL FRAMEWORKS IN ALGERIA, EGYPT, JORDAN, LIBYA, MOROCCO AND TUNISIA

OECD
BETTER POLICIES FOR BETTER LIVES

Please cite this publication as:
OECD (2017), *Women's Economic Empowerment in Selected MENA Countries: The Impact of Legal Frameworks in Algeria, Egypt, Jordan, Libya, Morocco and Tunisia*, Competitiveness and Private Sector Development, OECD Publishing, Paris.
http://dx.doi.org/10.1787/9789264279322-en

ISBN 978-92-64-27931-5 (print)
ISBN 978-92-64-27932-2 (PDF)

Series: Competitiveness and Private Sector Development
ISSN 2076-5754 (print)
ISSN 2076-5762 (online)

Photo credits: Cover © design by Renaud Madignier

Corrigenda to OECD publications may be found on line at: *www.oecd.org/about/publishing/corrigenda.htm*.

Foreword

As governments around the world are increasingly conscious that inequalities have become one of the principal obstacles to growth, they also realise that the first step towards building more inclusive and prosperous societies is to achieve Gender equality. While it is first and foremost a matter of rights, all economies also stand to gain from empowering women to use their full economic potential as this directly impacts countries' competitiveness, productivity and social well-being. It is estimated that raising women's labour force participation rates worldwide to male levels could add USD 12 trillion, or 26%, to global GDP by 2025.

The challenge of closing the gender gap in economic participation is especially acute in the Middle East and North Africa (MENA). Despite having a growing pool of highly educated women who want to work, MENA still has the lowest female labour force participation rate in the world at an average of 24%, compared to around 60% in OECD economies, and the highest gender gap in entrepreneurship. Recognising the untapped promise of women in the region, in the aftermath of the 2011 uprisings, many MENA countries enacted ambitious measures to strengthen women's status, notably through constitutional and institutional reforms. Yet ensuring that legal reforms are successful in tackling de facto discrimination and generating concrete economic opportunities for women remains a challenge, both in the MENA region and around the world.

To help provide a clearer picture of the impact of legal and legislative frameworks on women's economic involvement, MENA governments and stakeholders tasked the MENA-OECD Competitiveness Programme with undertaking a comprehensive study, which resulted in this report: *Women's Economic Empowerment in Selected MENA Countries: The Impact of Legal Frameworks in Algeria, Egypt, Jordan, Libya, Morocco and Tunisia.*

The report draws upon extensive research, policy discussions at the international and national levels, and insights from local focus groups involving both women and men. The report recognises the considerable progress that the region has made towards empowering women and the progressive evolution of legal frameworks. However, it is also clear that family law and other legal provisions are having a detrimental impact on the effective empowerment of women. The report underlines that in moving forward, legal reform must be accompanied by determined implementation strategies to ensure real social change and greater gender equality. Better alignment of national laws with international commitments and constitutional provisions, and guaranteeing women's full access to justice, will be essential in further accelerating progress.

This report contributes to a growing body of OECD work aimed at fostering greater equality between genders. Besides our support to the G20 in monitoring the reduction of the Gender gap in labour force participation by 25% by 2025, the OECD Gender Initiative, the OECD Council Recommendation on Gender Equality in Education, Employment and Entrepreneurship, and the OECD Council Recommendation on Gender Equality in Public Life are all key pillars of this effort.

As we aim to build better policies for a better world, promoting approaches that can unleash the talent and dynamism of women in MENA and beyond will mean better lives for us all.

Angel Gurría

OECD Secretary-General

Acknowledgements

This report is the result of a collective effort. It has been prepared in the context of the MENA-OECD Women's Business Forum of the MENA-OECD Competitiveness Programme within the OECD's Middle East and Africa Division of the Global Relations Secretariat (GRS/MENA). The data for the report were collected between 2013 and 2015. Legislation in some countries may have changed since this period, and can be expected to change in the future; this should be taken into account during follow-up discussions. In addition, in Egypt, Jordan, Morocco and Tunisia, the draft country reports were shared with government representatives, some of whom organised nationwide inter-governmental consultations that not only enhanced the findings, but provided opportunities for advocacy exchanges.

The analysis builds on country reports prepared by consultants from Algeria, Egypt, Jordan, Libya, Morocco and Tunisia, reflecting the economic participation of women in the respective countries as well as the legal framework under which they operate. The findings were validated through exchanges with: *i)* members of national collectives created by the consultants to validate their work; *ii)* representatives of focus groups (see Annex A); and *iii)* feedback collected in some countries during domestic inter-governmental consultations. The methodology allowed the collection of unique and rich input subsequent to extensive desk research carried out in the six countries. Draft country reports and synthesis reports, including recommendations, were submitted to review and discussions during international consultations with experts from the OECD and the region. Experts from within and outside the OECD provided guidance and comments to further enrich the report.

At the OECD, Nicola Ehlermann led the project and drafted the report, with the collaboration of Vanessa Vallée. Carlos Conde provided strategic direction. Other members of the MENA-OECD team who contributed to the report include Fares Al Hussami, Arthur Pataud, Pilar Sanchez-Bella, Sophie Teyssier, Roger Fores Carrion, as well as Molka Abassi and Alessandra Caputo. The report benefitted from the valuable contributions of Nathalie Bernard-Maugiron, consultant and research director at the Institut de Recherche pour le Développement, and a first comparative review by Serena Romano, consultant and member of the OECD-MENA WBF.

The report on Algeria was prepared by Isma Hassani and Meriem Terki and benefitted from inputs from researchers in areas of human rights, entrepreneurs and business representatives, lawyers, religious representatives and experts in religious matters, and representatives working for government entities.

The report on Egypt was researched and drafted by Nora Alim, who consulted Saher Salla, a former Minister for Trade and Industry and former managing director of the CIB Banks; Alia El-Mahdi, Faculty of Economics and Political Science, Cairo University; Naglaa El-Adly, Head of International Co-operation, National Women's Council; Heba Handoussa, Managing Director, Egypt Network for Integrated Development (ENID); Neveen El Tahri, Founder and President of the Board of Directors of Delta Investment Holding Company;

Shereen El Shorbagi, Industrial Modernisation Centre (IMC); Ahmed Darwish, Industrial Training Council (ITC); and Abla Abdel Latif, Chair of the Specialised Presidential Council for Economic Development.

The report on Jordan was researched and drafted by Maali Qasem Khader, who benefitted from input from Maha Al Ali, a former Secretary General of the Ministry of Industry and Trade; Asma Khader, a former public spokesperson for Jordan; Hala Ghosheh, gender expert; Deema Bibi, CEO of Injaz; Lina Abu Nuwar, Director at KAFA; Nisreen Barakat, Managing Director of To Excel and a former Minister of Social Development; Reem Abu-Hassan, lawyer and human rights activist and a former Minister of Social Development; Salma Nims, Secretary General of the Jordanian National Commission for Women; Hind Al-Fayez, General Manager of Sama Amman Jawaher Media Agency and Sakher Ground Handling Services; Oraib Rantawi, Director General of Al Quds Centre for Political Studies; Wafa' Bani Mustafa, lawyer; Abeer Dababneh, Assistant Professor at the University of Jordan; Lina Hundaileh, CEO of Chocolography; and Orouba Sobouh, journalist and human rights activist.

The report on Libya was prepared by Hanan Elnuweisri and Inas Miloud and was submitted to Wasef Salem Albadrani, a human rights activist in civil society and manager of a number of private business companies; Fars Alkharaz, legal consulate and expert on Libyan labour law in a private company; Madiha Alnaas, masters' student in Gender and Middle East Studies and gender researcher; Rida Altbuli, women's rights activist and head of a Libyan women's organisation; Asma Sriba, member of the Libyan General National Congress and expert in the transitional laws of Libya; Muryha Abd Allah, lawyer and active member in women's organisations; and Khaled Endar, economist and project manager.

The report on Morocco was prepared by Fatiha Daoudi and Soraya Badraoui and benefitted from the input of Aicha Belarbi, professor and former ambassador; Chadia Laghrari of the Ministry of Solidarity; Driss Ksikes, sociologist, researcher and teacher; Hammad Kassal, economist; Karim Mouttaki, lawyer and President of the Juridical Commission of the CGEM (Confédération Générale des Entreprises du Maroc); and Driss Yazami, Chairman of the Advisory Council for Human Rights in Rabat.

The report on Tunisia was prepared by Mouna Tabei and Manel Dridi, who collected views from Soukeina Bouraoui, Director of the Centre of Arab Women for Training and Research (CAWTAR); Neila Chaabane, Professor of Public Law and former Secretary of State for Women and the Family and the Childhood; Leila Khaiat, CONECT; Boutheina Gribaa, project co-ordinator and former Director of the Centre de Recherches, d'Etudes, de Documentation et d'Iinformation sur la Femme (CREDIF); Leila Belkhiria, vice president of the National Chamber of Women Entrepreneurs; Mongia Nefzi, Professor of Islamic Studies at the University of Zitouna in Tunis; Chema Gargouri, Country Director of Women Enterprise for Sustainability/Institute of International Education; Rym Haloues, sociologist; Hajer Trabelsi, expert and consultant in the access-to-information field; Souhaima Ben Achour, Professor of Private Law and specialist in family law; Wahid Ferchichi, Professor of Law and specialist in human rights and individual freedoms; Sasabil Klibi, Professor of Law and legal consultant; Salwa Hamrouni, lecturer and consultant in law; and Norchene Ben Dahmane, Professor at the Institute of Higher Commercial Studies (IHEC).

Experts from outside and within the OECD reviewed the report during the summer 2016: Delphine Borione, Deputy Secretary General for Social and Civil Affairs in the Secretariat of the Union for the Mediterranean; Soukeina Bouraoui, Director of CAWTAR;

Margareta Davidson-Abdelli, Counsellor, Embassy of Sweden in Cairo; Neveen El Tahri, Founder and President of the Board of Directors of Delta Investment Holding Company and Co-Chair of the MENA-OECD Women's Business Forum; Maryse Guimond, Programme Manager at UN Women Regional Office for Arab States; Fatiha Hassouni, Programme Manager at Union for the Mediterranean; H.E. Birgitta Holst Alani, a former Ambassador of Sweden and Co-Chair of the MENA-OECD Women's Business Forum; Leila Khaiat, First Vice President of the Council of Arab Business Women; H.E. Inas Makkawy, Head of the Department of Family and Childhood at the Secretariat General of the Arab League; Aysen Önen, lawyer and Vice-President of the International Federation of Jurist Women; Emanuela Pozzan, Senior Regional Gender Equality at ILO Specialist Regional Office for Arab States; Serena Romano, gender expert; Muriel de Saint Sauveur, former Director of the International Marketing and Communication and Director of Diversity of the Mazars Group; within the OECD, a special thanks goes to Willem Adema, Senior Economist for Family, Gender, Housing Policies and Social Expenditure Statistics; Lucia Cusmano, Administrator at SME and Entrepreneurship Division; Emily Esplen, Policy Analyst, Gender Equality and Women's Rights; Elena Gentili, Policy Analyst and Gender Project Co-ordinator; Keiko Nowacka, Co-ordinator, Gender Project; and Angelica Salvi del Pero, Senior Advisor to the ELS Director. Mary Bortin edited the publication.

The project and report benefitted from financial support from the Swedish International Development Agency (SIDA).

Table of contents

Figures

Tables

Boxes

Acronyms and abbreviations

ADB	African Development Bank
AFEM	Association des Femmes chefs d'Entreprise du Maroc
BDS	Business Development Services
CAWTAR	Centre of Arab Women for Training and Research
CEACR	ILO Committee of Experts on the Application of Conventions and Recommendations
CEDAW	Convention on the Elimination of All Forms of Discrimination Against Women
EBRD	European Bank for Reconstruction and Development
EfE	Education for Employment
ICCPR	International Covenant on Civil and Political Rights
ICESCR	International Covenant on Economic, Social and Cultural Rights
IDRC	International Development Research Centre
IFC	International Finance Corporation
ILO	International Labour Organization
IMF	International Monetary Fund
LAS	League of Arab States
MENA	Middle East and North Africa
MSME	Micro, Small and Medium Enterprise
NGO	Non-governmental organisation
OECD	Organisation for Economic Co-operation and Development
SDGs	Sustainable Development Goals
SIGI	Social Institutions and Gender Index
SME	Small and Medium Enterprise
TAPR	Technical Assistance for Policy Reform
TEA	Total Early-stage Entrepreneurial Activity
UDHR	Universal Declaration of Human Rights
UIS	UNESCO Institute of Statistics
UN	United Nations

UNDP	United Nations Development Programme
UNESCO	United Nations Educational, Scientific and Cultural Organization
UNICEF	United Nations Children's Emergency Fund
UN Women	United Nations Entity for Gender Equality and the Empowerment of Women
WB	World Bank
WBES	World Bank Enterprise Survey
WBF	Women's Business Forum
WDI	World Development Indicators

Executive summary

Women's Economic Empowerment in Selected MENA Countries analyses the challenges facing Algeria, Egypt, Jordan, Libya, Morocco and Tunisia in their efforts to boost women's employment and entrepreneurship, and offers policy recommendations for governments moving forward. It focuses on four main areas: Chapter 1 provides an overview of women's economic participation in the six countries; Chapter 2 examines international and constitutional provisions and women's access to justice; Chapter 3 analyses the impact of family law on women's empowerment; and Chapter 4 considers labour law in relation to women's rights as employees and entrepreneurs.

Women's participation in the labour market and entrepreneurship

Women remain an untapped potential factor for growth, competitiveness and inclusive social development in Algeria, Egypt, Jordan, Libya, Morocco and Tunisia. Data show significant improvements in education in the six countries, but also suggest that these advances have not yet translated into closing the gender gap in economic participation. The percentage of employed women in the six countries is among the lowest in the world. Wage gaps between men and women persist in both the private and the public sectors, and vulnerable or informal employment is particularly high among women. Rates of enterprise creation and development by women are also very low compared to countries in other regions of the world.

Although the six countries have made progress in data collection, a lack of gender-disaggregated data on education and economic participation makes it difficult for governments to enact informed policies that support female employment and entrepreneurship and to monitor these policies on a systematic basis.

International and constitutional commitments and women's access to justice

The six countries have ratified key international conventions that promote gender equality and non-discrimination between women and men. In the wake of the 2011 uprisings and calls from citizens for greater gender equality, some countries adopted new constitutions and others amended their constitutions to better reflect their international commitments; they also committed to regional standards and adopted specific policies to reinforce their pledge to support women's empowerment. Effective implementation of these commitments requires that the constitutional changes be incorporated into national legal frameworks, and this is work in progress.

Empowering women to claim their legal rights also requires effective enforcement by the justice system. Women and men in the six countries have equal access to justice in principle, but in practice women face a number of hurdles. The courts do not always enforce the rules, the judiciary may lack knowledge of current principles and standards, women are often not aware of their rights and, even when they are, social norms and financial constraints may hinder them from going to court. The fact that few judges are women may also be a factor.

Family law and the legacy of gender roles

Alongside civil law, countries of the MENA region enforce personal status codes that regulate relations within the family. Legislators in the six countries have introduced changes to family law that aim to increase gender equality. However, gender-based differences persist in matters ranging from marriage and divorce to property rights, inheritance and even the freedom to leave the house for work or travel.

Discriminatory provisions within personal status codes have negative implications for women's autonomy and adverse effects on their economic security, social roles and self-confidence. This in turn affects their capacity to participate fully in public and economic life. Legislative change on family matters is needed to reflect guarantees towards women's empowerment contained in countries' new or amended constitutions. Full consideration must be given to women's right to inclusive access to the economy as well as agency in their personal lives when translating relevant constitutional articles into legal code.

Women's labour rights and entrepreneurship

Only very limited amendments have been made to the labour laws of the six countries in recent years and no changes have been introduced subsequent to the adoption of the new constitutions. Similarly, with regard to entrepreneurship, there have not been any major reforms to the legal elements affecting the establishment, management or development of businesses; however, these laws are generally considered gender neutral.

Yet women face gender-specific challenges in both the workplace and entrepreneurship in areas ranging from recruitment and remuneration to social benefits and retirement. Some provisions aimed at protecting women impose restrictions or additional costs on private employers. Maternity leave and early retirement for women can affect their earnings and pensions. Women entrepreneurs face difficulties in accessing finance for their businesses and often lack the work experience and networks acquired by men. Sexual harassment and a lack of adequate and secure transportation can also impede women's participation in the economy.

Key actions

Governments can build on the progress already achieved through policy changes designed to foster women's economic empowerment. Key measures include:

- **Understanding the impact of gender inequality**: Gender-disaggregated data on education and economic activities are needed in order to enact informed policies on a systematic basis.
- **Implementing international commitments**: International conventions on gender equality and related commitments need to be embedded in national legal systems and enforced through effective monitoring.
- **Improving access to justice**: Knowledge of international conventions should be made an integral part of legal education in order to reinforce awareness of women's

rights among judges and legal professionals, and efforts are needed to strengthen women's awareness of their rights.

- **Making progress on family law**: Personal status codes need to be harmonised with the principles of gender equality and non-discrimination in line with national conventions and international commitments.
- **Strengthening gender equality in the labour market**: Labour laws need updating to combat discrimination against women in all types of work and throughout their working lives, and monitoring and sanctioning should be reinforced to bridge gaps between labour laws and practices.

A more detailed list of recommendations is available in the following "Assessment and Recommendations" section.

Assessment and recommendations to foster women's economic empowerment in selected MENA countries

This chapter provides an overview of the report's key findings on aspects critical to boosting women's economic empowerment in Algeria, Egypt, Jordan, Libya, Morocco and Tunisia. The report offers insights into women's labour market participation and entrepreneurship across the six countries, takes stock of countries' international and constitutional commitments to gender equality, and looks at women's access to justice. It examines the existing legal frameworks governing women's work as employees and entrepreneurs and assesses the impact of family law and traditional gender roles on outcomes. It also provides a succinct list of policy recommendations to support governments in their ongoing reform efforts to build more prosperous and inclusive societies by unleashing the economic potential of women.

Building inclusive societies is a high priority for the governments of Algeria, Egypt, Jordan, Libya, Morocco and Tunisia. In the aftermath of the 2011 uprisings, governments and non-governmental actors underscored the need for a clear picture on legislative frameworks and their impact on women's economic involvement. The six countries have amended or adopted new constitutions since 2011 that incorporate the principles of gender equality or non-discrimination. They recognise that the participation of women in the economy is key for growth and shared prosperity. This recognition at the constitutional level sends a strong and encouraging signal. As it is incorporated and implemented through the domestic legal framework, it will facilitate women's involvement in the economy.

The litmus test then lies in how legal progress translates into improvements on the ground. In the context of the unprecedented political, social and economic transformations since 2011, the MENA-OECD Competitiveness Programme undertook a review of the legal frameworks in the six countries with a view to determining their impact on women's economic involvement. This work was initiated after previous research by the OECD-MENA Women's Business Forum on the institutional framework and on key policy measures supporting women's entrepreneurship in the MENA region, including access to finance, business development services, networks and information. The first consultation, which determined the interest in engaging in this review, was held in December 2011 with government and private-sector representatives as well as parliamentarians.

The data for the report were mostly collected between 2013 and 2015 with additions, when available, up to mid-2016. Legislation in some countries may have changed since this period, and can be expected to change in the future. Such instances should be considered and factored in during any follow-up discussions at the country level or in international fora. Eventually, this work may also call for a revised draft to acknowledge progress and impacts made.

This report provides a nuanced comparative analysis of the different rights set out in the national constitutions of the six countries, their personal status codes and their laws on labour, taxation and business. It offers policy recommendations for boosting women's employment and entrepreneurship through changes to legislative and institutional frameworks. The recommendations are general and will need tailoring to the particular context of each country. This will call for more discussions at the national level to take account of the strengths and particularities of each economic, legal and institutional situation.

It is noteworthy that no country in the world has achieved full gender equality. Progress has been slow and uneven, and challenges persist across the globe. Legal and institutional barriers remain in many countries beyond the MENA region. For instance, women in over 100 countries covered by the Social Institutions and Gender Index (SIGI) still face legal and other forms of discrimination in their access to land and property, and 77 countries have inadequate legislation addressing domestic violence (OECD Development Centre, 2014).

Women's participation in the labour market and entrepreneurship

Gender equality is a fundamental driver for more inclusive and equitable societies, and in particular women's economic empowerment through economic participation as employees or entrepreneurs. Women's economic involvement promotes good use of skills and talent and increases social cohesion. The participation of women in the economy is indispensable for promoting global well-being, reducing poverty and combating inequality. In addition, women's economic independence increases their autonomy and ability to make decisions over critical areas of their lives, and enhances their economic and social status.

Data show significant improvements in education in the six countries. The data also suggest, however, that these advances have not yet translated into closing the gender gap in employment or entrepreneurship. A lack of gender-disaggregated data makes it difficult to provide a precise picture of women's and men's economic contributions. Yet it is clear that the economic participation of women in these countries is among the lowest in the world. A striking gap exists between labour supply and demand, leading to high unemployment, particularly among young educated women. Many women turn to vulnerable or informal employment, resulting in poor earnings and low-quality jobs. Far fewer women than men become entrepreneurs, and most of those who do create micro-firms that contribute little to formal employment, value added or productivity growth.

Governments of the six countries are encouraged to:

- Produce more gender-disaggregated data on education and economic activities in order to enact informed policies on a systematic basis.
- Assess the impact of policies that support female employment and entrepreneurship and identify the determinants of female labour market participation.

International and constitutional commitments and women's access to justice

Algeria, Egypt, Jordan, Libya, Morocco and Tunisia have ratified the United Nations Convention on the Elimination of All Forms of Discrimination Against Women (CEDAW) and core International Labour Organisation conventions that promote gender equality and non-discrimination between women and men. However, some reservations introduced by the countries have not yet been lifted and still affect the legal impacts of CEDAW. The countries have also committed to regional standards on gender equality and non-discrimination. Their new or amended constitutions since 2011 include provisions in support of gender equality or non-discrimination that strengthen the status of women and set the basis for their more balanced involvement in the economy. In light of this progress, governments could engage in further efforts to strengthen alignment with international instruments and ensure equal access to economic opportunities for women and men.

Access to justice and the enforcement of legal provisions are essential for gender equality. While women in the six countries have access to courts in principle, they face various barriers in practice, from lack of knowledge among judges of current standards to slack enforcement by courts of law and a deficit of women judges. Women themselves are often not aware of their rights, and social norms and financial constraints may discourage them from going to court.

In light of their efforts to work towards equality and further women's economic integration, the governments of the six countries may wish to continue to translate the progress made in their constitutions into all sets of laws in order to develop a coherent legislative environment that enhances the active role of women in the economy. They are also encouraged to work towards ensuring effective enforcement of the legal framework in order to ensure equality and non-discrimination among all citizens, notably in view of changing social attitudes, and to challenge discriminatory social norms and practices.

Governments are encouraged to:

- Lift their reservations to CEDAW and ratify the additional protocol, if they have not already done so, and incorporate a definition of gender-based discrimination, and an explicit prohibition of such discrimination, into the constitution and other relevant domestic legislation, in line with CEDAW's Article 1, when this has not yet been done.

- Ensure that international conventions and related commitments are incorporated into the constitution and embedded in the national legal system.
- Ensure the application of constitutional provisions that encourage women's involvement in political and economic activities and ensure diversity in those activities, including in the judiciary through a stronger participation of women judges; develop policies that promote equality in these domains; and monitor implementation of the principle of gender equality.
- Reinforce knowledge among judges, magistrates, lawyers and other legal professionals about international conventions that the government has ratified by making the conventions an integral part of legal education and training.
- Take measures to eliminate gender stereotyping, including awareness raising and capacity building for all actors of the justice system, and incorporate a legal culture supportive of gender equality and non-discrimination in all aspects of the justice system.
- Create a legal, social and political environment that promotes and supports access to justice by women, including through broad legal empowerment and legal-aid services at an affordable price; where not yet in place establish courts competent for minor litigation of relatively low value (small-claims courts) with simplified procedures; reinforce control and monitoring mechanisms to ensure legislation is implemented.
- Consider signing up to the 2013 OECD Council Recommendation on Gender Equality in Education, Employment and Entrepreneurship and the 2015 OECD Council Recommendation on Gender Equality in Public Life.

Family law and the legacy of gender roles

A striking difference remains between the countries' modernised constitutional norms and their personal status laws, which regulate relations within the family and are not gender neutral. Under these laws, which are based to varying degrees on religion, women do not share the same rights as men to pursue a profession, engage in travel or head a family. This affects economic outcomes and the application of egalitarian employment and entrepreneurship provisions. Discussions at the national and international levels testify to the fact that the personal status laws influence social values.

The six countries have introduced some reforms to their personal status laws in light of international standards and with due regard to new economic and social considerations. However, legal differentiation between women and men persists in relation to marriage, decision making, wealth, divorce, filiation and inheritance. This has a major bearing on the implementation of other economic laws and public policies. It limits women's autonomy and has wider social consequences.

With a view to greater equality and social justice, governments are encouraged to:

- Ensure that family law is in line with the principles outlined in international commitments and the country's constitution, and in particular that the personal status code is harmonised with the principle of gender equality and does not include provisions that are discriminatory in nature.

- Ensure an equitable distribution of duties between spouses and include a woman's right to work and travel without her husband's consent in legislative texts and/or promote the opportunity for women to include beneficial clauses in their marriage contract, such as the right to work and travel.
- Support the application of community property between spouses and allow women equal rights to assets acquired during the marriage in the event of divorce.
- Reconsider inheritance laws to ensure gender equality and encourage bequests between spouses or between parents and their heirs and follow Jordan's example and freeze a woman's share of the inheritance so that she is protected from being forced to renounce her inheritance rights.
- Raise awareness of the hardships women face within the current structures, in particular in the case of divorce, and improve their protection and rights, for instance allowing mothers to hold the status of "head of the family" or improve enforcement mechanisms.
- Create an expert task force to examine the economic impact of family law provisions, and develop recommendations on legal reforms that would help women engage more in the economic sphere. The task force could also examine whether and how men's high level of responsibility could negatively impact countries' competitiveness.

Women's labour rights and entrepreneurship

The principles of non-discrimination and equality are stated in the labour codes of the six countries, but various provisions of labour law differentiate between men and women. Although international and domestic laws prohibit discrimination in the recruitment process, working conditions and remuneration, these norms are not always respected in practice. Regulations that are intended to protect women may unintentionally bar them from certain types of work or from engaging in certain industries. For instance, regulations related to childcare are associated only with working women, whereas social benefits are almost exclusively paid to men. Early-retirement provisions can reduce women's time in paid work, leading to gender disparities in the workplace and affecting career profiles and earnings. It is also noteworthy that the labour laws do not cover all categories of workers, nor all types of work and sectors. These gaps leave workers vulnerable and encourage informal work conditions, an impediment affecting women's participation in the formal labour force.

Women entrepreneurs also face gender-specific difficulties that may hinder them from establishing, managing or developing a business. For instance, although laws regulating enterprise development are gender neutral, personal status laws make distinctions between men and women that create barriers to women's access to finance. Social norms embedded in the personal status laws have an impact on women's overall economic independence, assertiveness and assessment of their capacities for entrepreneurship.

These provisions create inequalities among men and women in their access to job opportunities and career perspectives. Violence and sexual harassment, as well as a lack of security infrastructure in public transportation, can further hinder women's participation in the economy.

With this in mind, governments are encouraged to:

- Combat gender-related discrimination against women in all types and sectors of work and throughout all stages of their working life, including recruitment, access to promotion and senior management positions, and pay relative to male colleagues; apply international standards concerning the jobs from which women are restricted (so-called "hazardous" jobs or jobs with night hours); strengthen monitoring and sanctioning mechanisms to bridge existing gaps between labour laws and practices.
- Ensure that the labour code covers all categories of workers, all types of work and all sectors in order to reduce informality and protect all employees, and in particular women.
- Review maternity leave and child care provisions to dissociate the perceived costs of childrearing from women as much as possible: ensure that employers do not bear maternity leave or childcare costs directly by offering publicly supported, indirect financing mechanisms (e.g. social insurance funds) and state-supported childcare solutions; reform tax and social-benefits systems to provide equal financial incentives for both parents to work; promote equal sharing of family responsibilities through parental leaves in line with ILO recommendations.
- Enact regulations and/or provide incentives for employers to support part-time employment, remote working and flexible hours for both genders in order to help reconcile working hours and family life.
- Guarantee women a safe environment at and on their way to work by: ensuring strict enforcement of sexual harassment regulations and punishing offenders; allowing victims to leave their jobs if desired while maintaining their rights to dismissal compensation; penalising harassment in public places; and enhancing women's mobility by improving transportation and infrastructure.
- Foster a greater role for women in economic decision making through affirmative-action programmes or measures such as temporary quotas or targets in public and private governance structures, e.g. leadership and management positions as well as company-board positions; complement such measures by leadership-development opportunities for women and men to give equal access to senior posts through career counselling services, coaching and mentoring.
- Reduce barriers to women's entrepreneurship through policies that: support equal access to finance, including the amendment of current legislation; prohibit discrimination based on sex or marital status; foster the development of credit registries and credit bureaus; encourage financial institutions to take different sorts of collateral into consideration; develop guarantee mechanisms to compensate for women's limited assets; support the development of alternative funding sources; and increase women's financial education.
- Move towards pension-age parity (public/private and by gender) by encouraging female employees to prolong the age at which they retire so that they may build up longer contribution periods; launch awareness-raising campaigns, information centres, special programmes for rural women and spaces dedicated to women's pensions on government web sites to help women understand the implications for their pensions of working less than full time or retiring early.

Chapter 1

Women's participation in the labour market and entrepreneurship in selected MENA countries

This chapter presents an overview of women's educational attainment, participation in the labour market and involvement in entrepreneurship in the six countries under review – Algeria, Egypt, Libya, Jordan, Morocco and Tunisia. It examines women's engagement in the economies of the six countries as compared to men's participation as well as to women's economic involvement in other parts of the world. The chapter also seeks to better understand the main features defining women's economic status and the different characteristics of men and women in employment and entrepreneurship.

Introduction

There is a striking gap between women's improved education and their limited participation in economic activities in Algeria, Egypt, Jordan, Libya, Morocco and Tunisia.

Despite the substantial narrowing of the gender gap in education, the percentage of women in the total employed population in the six countries is among the lowest in the world, at 17.9%, compared with the world average of 47.1% (World Development Indicators, 2014). Female labour-force participation in these countries ranges from 15.4% in Algeria to 30% in Libya. At the same time, a dramatic gap between labour supply and demand in the female workforce has been creating high levels of unemployment, in particular among young educated women. Vulnerable or informal employment is particularly high among women, resulting in poor earnings and low-quality jobs. In entrepreneurship, the gender gap in the Middle East-North Africa region is the greatest in the world, with around 12% of adult women and 31% of adult men working as entrepreneurs (GEM, MENA Regional Report, 2012).

The inclusion of skilled women in the economy should expand the talent pool, providing for a more productive and diversified economy that can engage in innovation and compete globally. Women's economic participation provides them with resources that allow them to realise their personal aspirations, and to support their families, leading to increased well-being among women, men and children. Gender parity is not only a fundamental human right but also a critical economic opportunity for countries. Research using the SIGI 2014 results reveals that gender-based discrimination in social institutions is significant and represents a cost of USD 575 billion for the MENA region (Ferrant and Kolev, 2016). Addressing the obstacles to women's and girls' empowerment could benefit the economy as a whole.

In order to understand the impact of gender inequality, data and evidence are crucial. National statistics offices have made progress collecting gender-disaggregated data, which are used by international agencies to develop internationally comparable data series and indicators. Regrettably, the overall availability of gender-disaggregated data in the MENA region is still limited. More detailed gender-disaggregated data at the national and regional levels should be collected and made available to better inform policy making and help monitor progress.

Towards gender equality in education

Since independence, education in the six countries has been declared a guaranteed right and literacy rates have significantly improved.[1] The literacy gap between women and men has also narrowed. By 2012, female literacy was almost equivalent to the male rates attained in 1994. It had reached over 70% in Tunisia and almost 100% in Jordan. But the gap is still significant in some countries. In Morocco only 57% of women were literate, compared to 76% of men, and in Egypt only 65% of women could read, compared to 81% of men (Figure 1.1).

The gender gap in participation at different school levels has also narrowed in the six countries. Girls' primary enrolment tends to be below that of boys – about 5% lower in Algeria and Morocco and roughly 2% in Jordan and Egypt. In secondary education, all countries except Morocco have 100% enrolment rates for both boys and girls. Gaps in participation in tertiary enrolment have narrowed as well. Jordan and Libya are close to gender parity, while Egypt and Morocco still face a gender gap of roughly 10% in favour of men. In contrast, female enrolment rates in Algeria and Tunisia tend to be about 50% higher than those of men (UIS, 2016).

Figure 1.1. **Evolution of female and male literacy rates (%)**

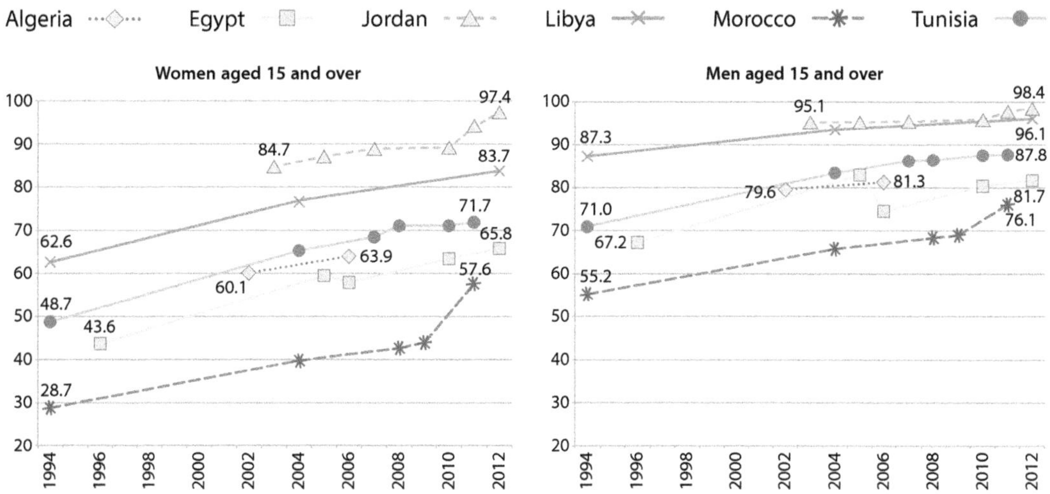

Source: World Bank (2016), World Bank Development Indicators database; http://databank.worldbank.org/data/reports.aspx?source=world-development-indicators.

Nevertheless, gender disparities in education persist across and within countries in terms of total years of schooling. The average length of total schooling is 1.2-2 times higher among men than women except in Libya, where women study almost one year more than men (Figure 1.2). Differences exist between urban and rural areas because wealth is an important factor shaping educational attainment. Fields of specialisation also tend to differ between males and females (WB, 2007). Women concentrate on education, arts or humanities, and are less represented in engineering or law, although progress in these fields has been noted in recent years.

Figure 1.2. **Average total years of schooling by gender for people over 25 in 2010 (%)**

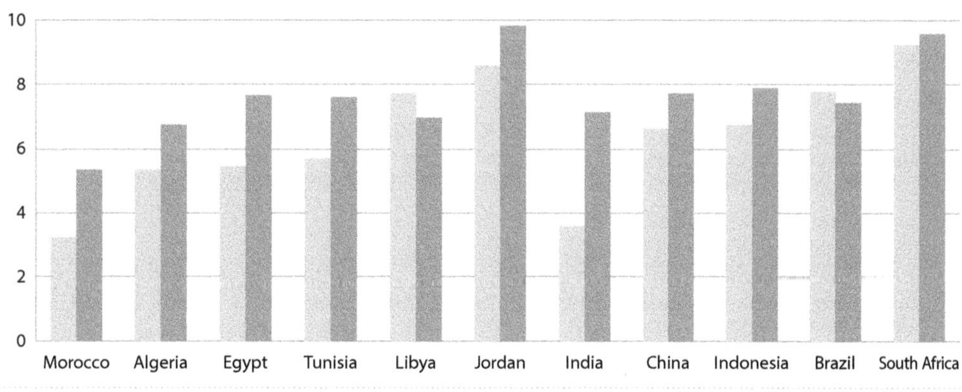

	Morocco	Algeria	Egypt	Tunisia	Libya	Jordan	India	China	Indonesia	Brazil	South Africa
Women	3.23	5.31	5.44	5.7	7.73	8.58	3.56	6.61	6.71	7.8	9.27
Men	5.33	6.71	7.68	7.6	6.97	9.8	7.15	7.7	7.88	7.45	9.6

Source: Barro, R. J. and J. W. Lee. 2013. Barro-Lee dataset of Educational Attainment. www.barrolee.com, Accessed August 2015.

Despite government efforts in the six countries leading to a strong drop in illiteracy rates, and important progress in women's educational attainment in all school cycles, this has not translated into higher women's labour-force participation and entrepreneurship.

Restricted female labour force participation

Women in the MENA region remain an untapped resource for the economy. While women represent around 49% of the total population, their participation in the labour force is very low (WB gender statistics, 2016). In Jordan and Algeria only about 16% of women older than 15 participate in the labour force, whereas in Egypt, Libya, Morocco and Tunisia it ranges from 25% to 32% (Figure 1.3). The average female labour force participation rate for OECD countries is 50.9%.[2] In contrast, men's participation in the labour force in the six countries reached 70% or more in 2014, only slightly below other emerging economies (WDI, 2016).

Figure 1.3. **Female labour force participation (15+)**

1990-2005-2014 (%)

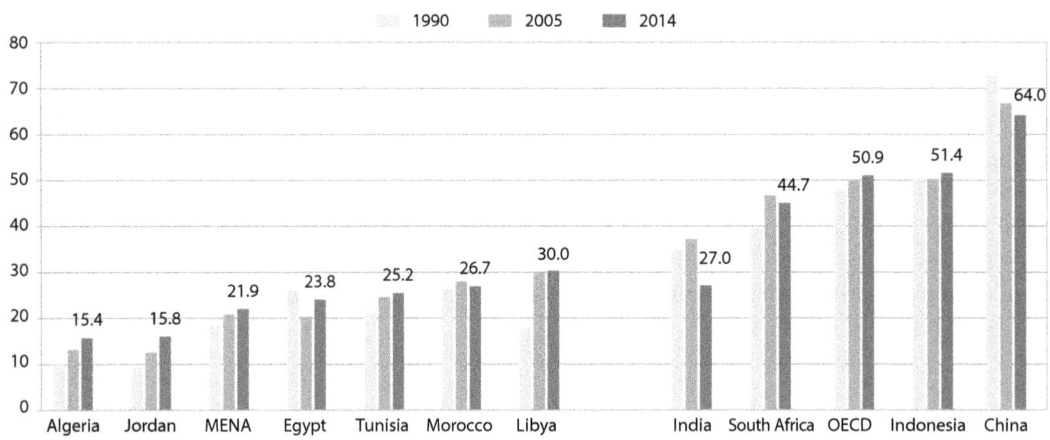

Source: World Bank (2016), World Bank Development Indicators database, http://databank.worldbank.org/data/reports.aspx?source=world-development-indicators.

Note: Female labour force participation refers to the percentage of women older than 15 years who are economically active. According to the World Bank data, the MENA region includes the following countries: Algeria, Bahrain, Djibouti, Egypt, Iran, Iraq, Israel, Jordan, Kuwait, Lebanon, Libya, Morocco, Oman, Qatar, Saudi Arabia, Syrian Arab Republic, Tunisia, United Arab Emirates, West Bank and Gaza, and Yemen.

The female-to-male labour force participation ratio in the six countries ranges from 21.2% in Algeria to 39.3% in Libya, compared to the average of 74.8% in OECD countries (Figure 1.4). The gap between male and female participation was reduced during the 1990s, but this progress slowed afterwards. Between 2005 and 2014, the gap continued narrowing only in the countries that had been lagging behind: Algeria, Egypt and Jordan.[3] This deceleration can be partly explained by the expansion of secondary and tertiary education, which considerably reduced the labour force participation rate among the youngest. In Morocco, for instance, labour force participation of women aged 15-24 decreased by 12 percentage points from 1999 to 2013 (OECD findings).

Figure 1.4. **Female-to-male labour force participation ratios**

1990-2005-2014 (%)

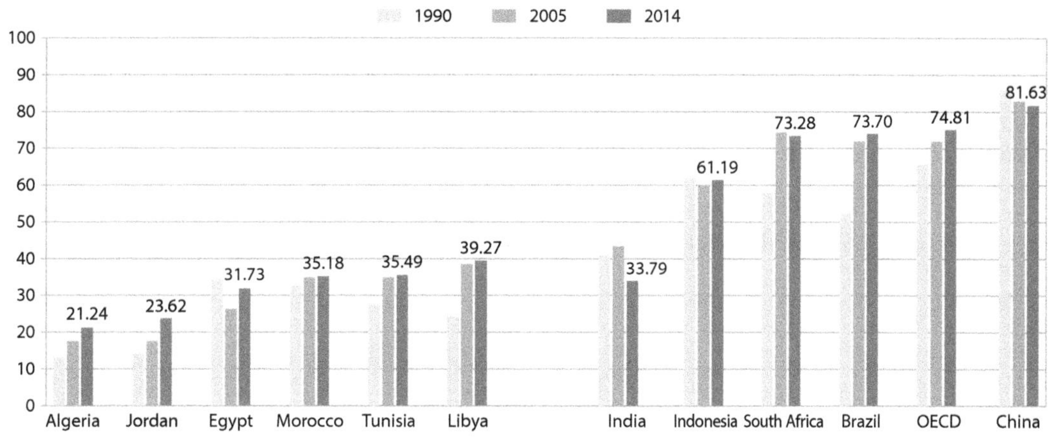

Source: Labour force participation ratio is the proportion of the population aged 15 and older that is economically active: all people who supply labour for the production of goods and services during a specified period. Female-to-male labour force participation measures how many women are active in the labour force for every 100 men.

Note: World Bank (2016), World Bank Development Indicators database, Washington, DC, http://databank.worldbank.org/data/reports.aspx?source=world-development-indicators.

Women's employment in the public and private sectors

In the MENA region, the public sector has traditionally employed the majority of women. In 2013, the percentage of working women employed in the public sector was 91% in Libya, 61% in Algeria and more than 50% in Egypt.[4] Public sector employment has been preferred by women as it is considered more socially acceptable (Sayre and Hendy, 2013). The public sector is associated with higher job security, a safer work environment, better reconciliation with family duties (Assaad, 2014). It is also perceived to provide higher salaries and benefits, particularly at the local level and certainly for entry-level jobs.

Within the public sector, women tend to work in what have traditionally been considered female domains, in particular in the education and service sectors. In Morocco in 2009, women accounted for around 50% of employees in the ministries of Health and Social Affairs, but only 4% in the General Directorate for Civil Protection and 6% in the General Directorate for National Security (OECD, 2014b: 164).

Overall, women's participation rate in the private sector is limited (Assaad, 2014). Women continue to work in a more restricted range of professions than men. Independently of educational attainment, women are likely to remain in low-pay jobs with few responsibilities and are under-represented in high-level managerial positions or on boards of directors. They are also frequently employed in the informal sector.

Labour market dynamics in the region over the past decades have not favoured female labour force participation. On one hand, the number of available public sector jobs in the region declined with the Structural Adjustment Policies initiated in the 1980s. On the other, this decline was not compensated by a sufficient increase of jobs in the private sector – the MENA region has the world's lowest private-sector investment contribution to growth – and the majority of the region's investments were directed to low-skilled and capital-intensive sectors in which women's participation is lower.

Age-related women's labour force participation

As in most countries, women's labour force participation strongly increases between the ages of 15 and 29. After the age of 30, however, and in contrast to men, women's participation in the workforce decreases sharply (Algeria, Jordan, Libya and Tunisia) or progressively (Egypt and Morocco). This contrasts with OECD countries, where the number of women in the labour force declines somewhat in child-bearing years but increases again at a later age (Figure 1.5).

Figure 1.5. **Female labour force participation rates by age groups, 2013 (%)**

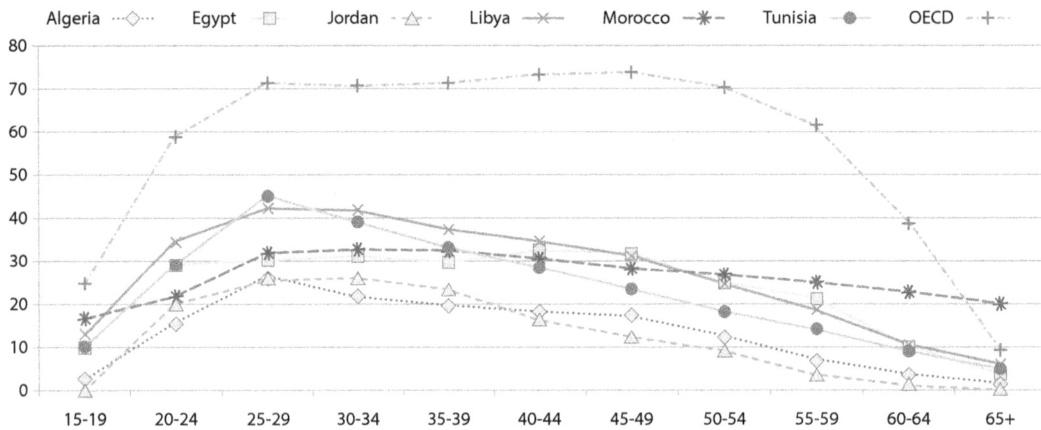

Source: International Labour Office (2016), ILOSTAT/ ILO database of labour statistics.

Education and labour force participation

As in other regions, women's propensity to participate in the workforce increases with their level of education (Mryyan, 2014). Working women across the six countries have a considerably higher level of education than their male peers, and also higher than women in the same age range who do not work. The 2014 data for Algeria show that 70% of women with a tertiary degree are working or actively trying to find a job, compared to 44% of those with vocational training and 7% who do not have any degree (ILO statistics, 2016). This pattern also holds true for Egypt, Morocco and Tunisia.[5] The proportion of educated women is higher within younger age groups, with the most educated between 20 and 29 years old.

In some MENA economies, women who leave the labour force after the age of 30 tend to be the most educated. In Jordan, for instance, the share of women dropping out of the labour force after 30 increases by 29 percentage points for those with a university education, while that of women with lower levels of education increases by no more than 7 percentage points (Sayre and Hendy, 2013).

Wage gaps

Pay gaps between men and women persist in the region, and the gap is generally higher in the private than in the public sector. Public sector salaries are regulated in terms of grades, seniority, etc., making discriminatory practices less explicit.

The gender pay gap varies considerably across the six countries. In 2007, the average pay gap in Egypt was estimated to be 25%, with particularly high disparities in the sectors of mining (72%), manufacturing (35%) and health and social work (25%) (Tijdens and Klaveren, 2012). The difference is significantly higher in the formal private sector (35-40%) than in the public sector (2%), which would further reinforce women's preference for the public sector (World Bank, 2014). Some studies argue that the Egyptian pay gap can be attributed mainly to "discrimination against women" and not to differences in human capital characteristics (Biltagy, 2014).

In Libya, the pay gap amounted to 7% in the public and 20% in the private sector (Elgazzar et al., 2015). In Jordan, on the other hand, the wage gap decreased considerably in 2011, to an hourly gender pay gap of 9% for the private sector and 5% for the public sector. This is lower than in OECD countries, where the average pay gap is about 15%. In the case of Jordan, the generally lower gender pay gap can potentially be explained by the fact that only a small and particularly educated share of women participate in the labour force, and that only some of them in turn are in paid employment. Thus, those remaining in the statistics show a higher level of education than for employed men on average (Sweidan, 2012).

One of the conclusions from the Moroccan focus group of jobseekers was that the pay gap is primarily due to women's lack of experience in negotiating and a tendency among women to accept whatever they are offered.[6] The high level and long duration of unemployment may also increase women's willingness to accept wages below those of their male colleagues.

Gender gaps in senior management positions and on boards of directors

The share of women in positions of high responsibility is low in both the public and private sectors. The average share of executive positions held by women in the public and private sectors combined was 14.8% in Tunisia, 12.8% in Morocco, 9.7% in Egypt, 5.1% in Jordan and 4.9% in Algeria (ILO, 2015a). This compares to 42.7% in the United States, 35.5% in Sweden, and 25.8% in Italy, with the lowest ranking OECD country being Korea at 11%.

In Tunisia, women are employed in jobs with lower qualifications than equally educated men (Stampini and Verdier-Chouchane, 2011). The under-representation of women in positions of high responsibility may be linked to the significant female drop-out rates from the labour force at a young age, as many such positions become accessible only with considerable work experience. The difficulty of attaining senior positions could be an additional factor dissuading women from entering or staying in the job market.

Female youth unemployment, underemployment and youth inactivity

The MENA region faces both the highest overall unemployment levels and the widest gender gap worldwide. In 2014, unemployment rates for young females ranged from 19.1% in Morocco to 69.2% in Libya, considerably high compared to an average of 16.2% in OECD countries (Figure 1.6). And while a gender gap in unemployment is almost non-existent in other emerging countries (India, Indonesia, China) or within the OECD, female unemployment rates were twice as high as those of men in Libya and Egypt, and in the overall MENA region.

Unemployment in the MENA region is particularly high among young adults aged 15 to 24. The unemployment ratio is 3.7 times higher for youth than adults, and it is higher than in the OECD or other regions of the world (ILO, 2015b). Despite the limited number of women in the region's labour market, unemployment rates among young women are nearly 50% higher than among young men. Female youth unemployment rates reach levels as high as 69.2% in Libya. In Egypt and Libya, female youth unemployment increased by more than 15 percentage points from 2010 to 2013, in Jordan it increased by 7 percentage points, whereas it remained roughly constant in Algeria, Tunisia and Morocco (ILO estimates).

Figure 1.6. **Youth unemployment and total unemployment rates by gender (15-24), 2014**

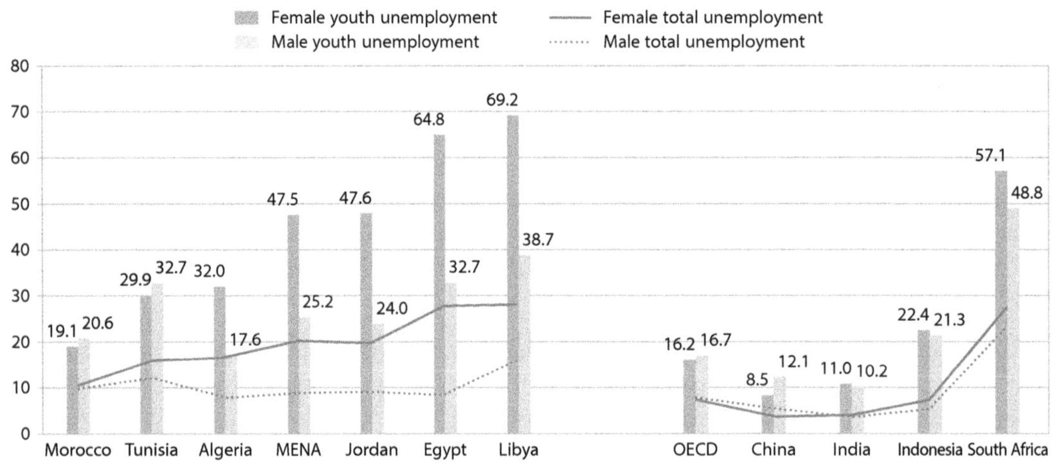

Source: World Bank (2016), World Bank Development Indicators database, http://databank.worldbank.org/data/reports.aspx?source=world-development-indicators.

Time-related underemployment is another issue for women in the region as it translates into a reduced income. Persons in time-related underemployment are those who are willing and able to work additional hours but who work fewer than the desired weekly hours of work. In some countries, women are much more vulnerable to time-related underemployment. In Egypt, 24% of working women worked fewer than 35 hours a week in 2012, compared with only 4% of working men. Women work mostly in the agricultural sector (60%) and manufacturing (17%). The higher share of time-related underemployment among women in Egypt may be linked to its bigger informal sector. In Morocco, on the other hand, and although the country has the highest share of vulnerable employment among the six countries, the percentage of part-time workers was 2-3% for both women and men (ILO Statistics).

Another way to assess young women's economic involvement is to measure their degree of inactivity by looking at the share of those who are not in education, employment or training (NEET). Nowhere is NEET higher for youth than in the Middle East and North Africa. Available country data for Egypt, Jordan and Tunisia show that the share of NEET youth aged 15 to 24 ranges between 30% and 25%. For young people up to the age of 29, the share increases to about 30-35%. In the three countries, NEET is much higher for young women than young men, with the highest disparities in Egypt (ETF, 2014).

As noted above, working women in the six countries have a higher education level than men and women of working age in general. It appears that unemployed women are also better educated than unemployed men. In Tunisia, Egypt and Morocco, women with a tertiary education are more likely to be unemployed than those with lower levels of education.[7] In Algeria and Jordan, 52% and 65% of unemployed women respectively are university graduates, compared with only 11% and 21% among men (ILO, 2016).

Vulnerable and informal employment

When no employment opportunities are offered in the formal sector, women in the MENA region seem more likely than men to work in informal and unpaid employment (Berniell and Sánchez-Páramo, 2011). Vulnerable employment, defined as the share of unpaid family workers and own-account workers (ILO), is higher among women than men in Egypt and Morocco (Figure 1.7).

Figure 1.7. **Female and male vulnerable employment (as % of total male/female employment), latest available data by country**

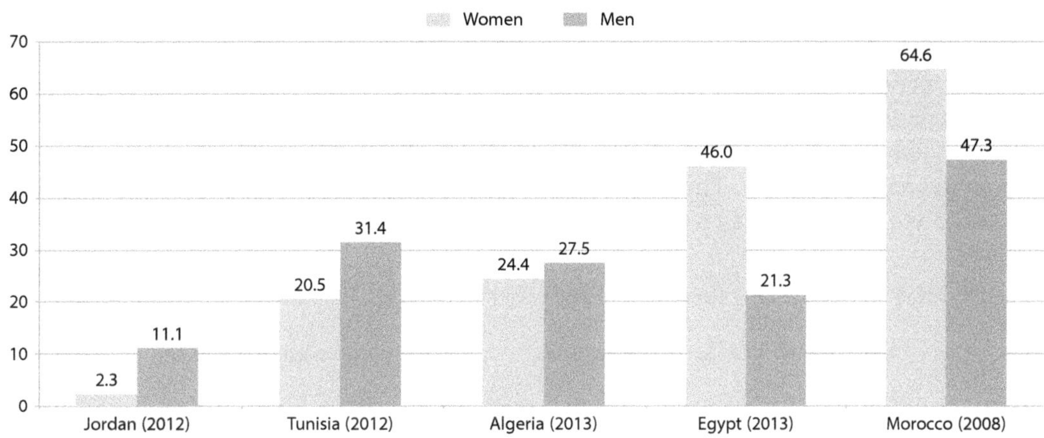

Source: World Bank (2016), World Bank Development Indicators database, http://databank.worldbank.org/data/reports.aspx?source=world-development-indicators.

Egypt illustrates the labour market dynamics created by MENA's declining public sector since the mid-1980s. The share of informal employment among new job seekers doubled from 1975 to 2005, with informal employment defined as work performed without any labour contract, job security or social benefits (Assaad and Barsoum, 2007). Job guarantees for university graduates, now obsolete, incentivised job-seeking women to look for work in the private sector.

Participants in the Moroccan focus group noted that a potential explanation for the high rate of vulnerable employment among women in Morocco is their extensive participation in the agricultural sector in rural areas. In fact, 98% of women employed in rural areas lack medical coverage, compared to 53% employed in urban areas (Moroccan Ministry of Energy and Mines dataset, 2012). In urban areas, women are more concentrated than men in small business, which tends to have more precarious work conditions – 45% and 40%, respectively (High Commission of Planning, Morocco dataset, 2013). Moreover, female employment in the informal sector is characterised by a predominance of unpaid care work and a vulnerable job status.

Around 12% of adult women in MENA are entrepreneurs compared with 31% of men, the largest gender gap across the regions of the world (GEM MENA regional report, 2012). However, the lack of gender-disaggregated data makes it difficult to evaluate and monitor female entrepreneurship in the MENA region.

The Global Entrepreneurship Monitor (GEM) provides information on individuals' entrepreneurial activities (with little attention to the characteristics of the enterprise, e.g. size or legal status), according to three phases: 1) being involved in a nascent business; 2) owning a new business that is less than three-and-a-half years old; and 3) owning an established business that is more than three-and-a-half years old.

About 34% of entrepreneurs involved in nascent enterprises in MENA are women, compared with 42% in other emerging economies. This drops to 22% during the early stage of the business life course, and the decrease continues to just 17% of established businesses. The proportion is far lower than in other emerging and developed economies.

The rate of total early-stage entrepreneurial activity (TEA) measures the percentage of the 18-to-64-year-old population involved in an entrepreneurial activity that is either a nascent (phase 1) or a new business (phase 2). While TEA gender gaps barely exist in other emerging economies (e.g. Indonesia, Malaysia, or Brazil), the gap is significant in the six countries under review (Figure 1.8). The largest difference between male and female TEA rates is shown in Egypt, where men make up around 86% of early-stage entrepreneurs and women the remaining 14%. The gap is smaller in Morocco, Algeria and Libya, where it is still twice as likely for a man to engage in an entrepreneurial activity.[8]

Figure 1.8. **Early stage entrepreneurial activity rate, GEM, 2015 (or latest available data)**

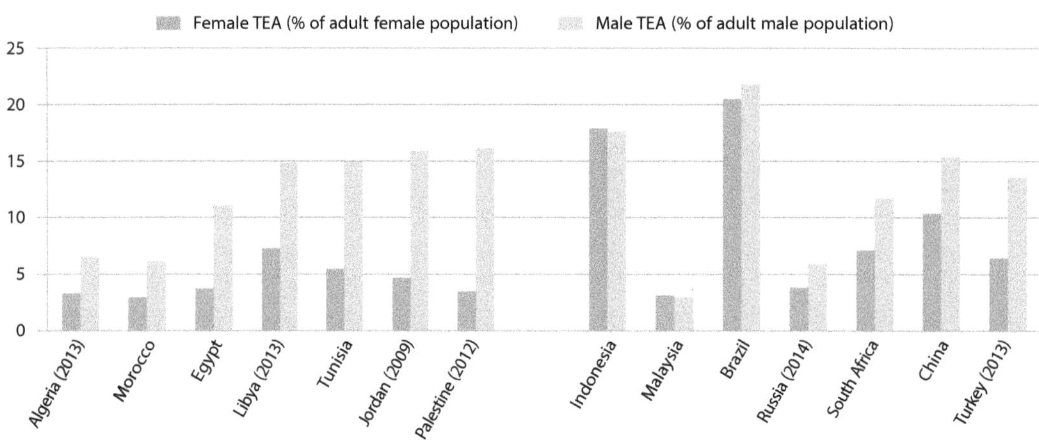

Source: Global Entrepreneurship Monitor (2015), Adult Population Survey Measures, 2015. www.gemconsortium.org/data.

Note: TEA refers to the combined total of adults actively trying to start a new business (nascent entrepreneurs) and adults already owning a young business fewer than 42 months old.

Characteristics of women entrepreneurs and their businesses

Women entrepreneurs in the MENA region tend to have a lower socio-economic profile than their male peers (OECD, 2014a; OECD/IDRC, 2013). Women entrepreneurs generally come from households with lower income levels and have fewer resources to set up a business. Women who own and manage ventures have lower education levels than men, although they are more educated than the average MENA woman. They also have much less work experience, given their overall low level of labour force participation, affording them fewer opportunities to acquire skills, identify potential business opportunities and set aside savings. Women's limited work experience before starting a business is likely to drive a higher attrition rate, since business experience is critical for success (OECD/IDRC, 2013).

Women also differ from men in their attitudes and aspirations towards entrepreneurship. Across countries with available data (Algeria, Egypt, Tunisia), women have a higher fear of failure, believe less in their own capabilities, are less connected to other entrepreneurs and are less optimistic about potential business opportunities (Figure 1.9).

Figure 1.9. **Entrepreneurial perceptions of women and men in Algeria, Egypt and Tunisia, 2012 (%)**

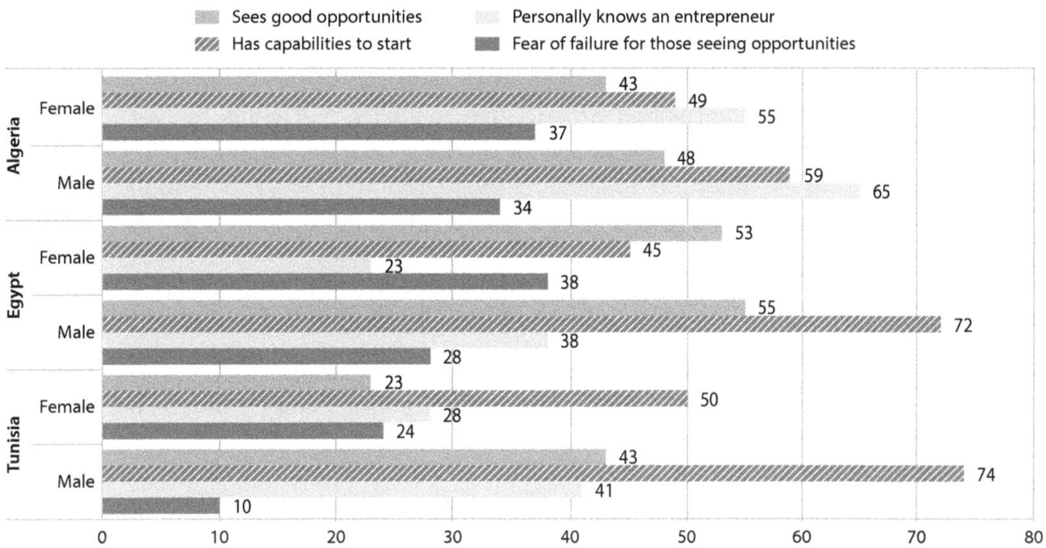

Source: Global Entrepreneurship Monitor (2013), Global Entrepreneurship Monitor, 2012 Women's Report, www.babson.edu/Academics/centers/blank-center/global-research/gem/Documents/GEM%202012%20Womens%20Report.pdf.

Note: Data for Jordan, Libya and Morocco is not available.

Although the data is not disaggregated by gender, several factors seem to indicate that more women than men are driven to entrepreneurship by necessity. In the MENA region, the share of entrepreneurial activity resulting from "necessity" rather than "opportunity" tends to be high and has been increasing over the past years (GEM, 2013).[9] In Egypt, for instance, the share of men and women entrepreneurs driven by necessity rose from 20% in 2008 to 75% in 2010. At the same time, the percentage of women-owned and managed enterprises also increased (OECD, 2014a: 60). In Tunisia, the share of men and women driven by necessity increased from roughly 22% in 2009 to 35% in 2012 (GEM country report 2012).

Women entrepreneurs typically value the flexibility that comes with being their own boss. They are more likely than men to cite work/life balance as their motivation for becoming an entrepreneur rather than growth or profits. And yet, women consistently rate self-employment as being less feasible than men do because of cultural attitudes and higher perceived barriers.

Female-owned enterprises are more prevalent in consumer-oriented sectors and businesses like health and beauty, retail, hospitality and social services. Start-up costs and entry barriers are relatively low in these areas, but they also generally offer limited development potential. Women are less present in the transforming and extractive sectors (OECDa, 2014). In Egypt, for instance, female-owned enterprises tend to be concentrated in the trade (50%), manufacturing (22%), education and health sectors, while men's businesses are generally more diversified across the economy (GEM country report 2012).

Business ownership

Corporate ownership, defined as the presence of at least one woman among the owners of a business, can be an important element in promoting overall gender equality. The gender of the dominant shareholder in a company can be a key governance factor favouring diversity in leadership positions (Sekkat et al., 2015). For instance, the chief executive of firms with a female dominant shareholder has a significantly higher probability of being a woman than in other firms. The effect is more pronounced when the female shareholder holds a higher share of the capital (Sekkat et al., 2015).

In MENA economies, female participation in ownership is low compared with that of men, with significant variations among the countries.[10] Among the six countries reviewed, only in Tunisia, and to a lesser extent Morocco, do women have a relatively high participation in ownership (Figure 1.10). In Jordan and Egypt, female participation is weak, representing around 16% in 2013.[11] This compares with an average rate in OECD countries of around 35%, and with about 22% in Indonesia and 25% in Turkey.[12] On the other hand, participation in ownership does not necessarily imply a high share of income (e.g. a woman's formal participation in ownership of the firm of her husband).

Figure 1.10. **Firms with female participation in ownership (% of firms)**

2015 (or latest available data)

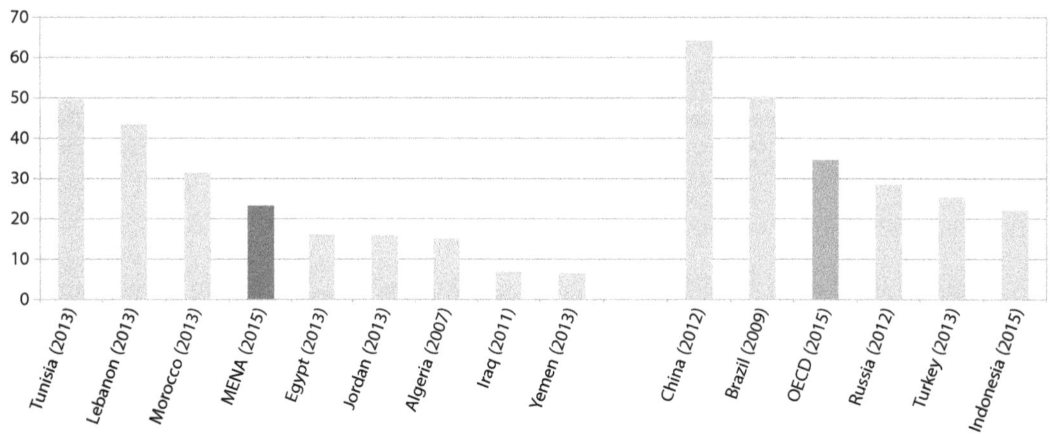

Source: World Bank (2016), World Bank Development Indicators database, http://databank.worldbank.org/data/reports.aspx?source=world-development-indicators.

Note: Firms with female participation in ownership' refers to the percentage of firms with a woman among the principal owners. Data for Libya is not available.

Conclusions

Women's economic participation remains limited in the six countries under review. These countries have among the lowest rates of female entrepreneurship and labour force participation globally, with large gender gaps. Vis-à-vis men, women are more likely to be in low-paid occupations, whether as employees or entrepreneurs, and are less likely to attain leadership positions. Although incomplete data prevent an in-depth analysis, it may be assumed that women resort to entrepreneurship by necessity given their limited opportunities for paid employment.

Such large gender gaps in employment and entrepreneurship cannot be explained by women's educational attainment, as all six countries have made important schooling gains and reduced the gender education gap in recent years. In the next chapters we will examine whether the legislative frameworks of the six countries contain provisions that hold back women's economic empowerment.

Recommendations

Governments are encouraged to:

- Produce more gender-disaggregated data on education and economic activities in order to enact informed policies on a systematic basis.
- Assess the impact of policies that support female employment and entrepreneurship and identify the determinants of female labour market participation.

Notes

1. In Jordan, the 1952 Constitution declared education compulsory and free of charge. The 1959 Constitution in Tunisia proclaimed equal access to education, which became compulsory in 1991. In Morocco, education for children aged 6 to 13 became compulsory in 1963. In Egypt, the 1971 Constitution established public education as compulsory and free of charge. In Algeria, education became obligatory in 1970. In Libya, education is compulsory and is free of charge at all levels, including advanced education.
2. According to the OECD standard age grouping (15-64), the female labour force participation rate is around 67%.
3. Jordan's increase in female labour force participation, and as a consequence, in the ratio of female-to-male labour force participation, might be due to a change in methodology after 2006, which made the female rate rise from 12% to 15% (Assaad and Hendy, 2012).
4. Egypt has traditionally had a large public sector, employing 80% of first job seekers in the mid-1970s (UNESCO, 2012). Today, the public sector remains the largest sector employing women, hiring 50% of all women in the labour force in 2012 (OECD findings).
5. In Morocco in 2012, only 14% of women with pre-primary education participated in the labour force, compared with 47% among women with post-secondary non-tertiary education. (ILO Statistics, 2016). Likewise, in Tunisia the most important share of women in the labour force has attained tertiary education, with a rate of 38.3%, against 19.1% for males, followed by females with secondary education (30%, against 37% for males), and with primary education (19.3%, against 32.9% for males) (Tunisia national census, 2014).
6. As part of the data collection process for this report, a series of focus groups was organised. For more information concerning the methodology and participant demography of the focus groups, see Annex A.
7. In 2015, the unemployment rate of women with a tertiary education was 41% and the average female unemployment rate was 15%, according to the Tunisian National Institute of Statistics. In Morocco in 2013, the unemployment rate for women with a *niveau supérieur* (high level of education) was above 25%, whereas that for a *niveau moyen* (middle level) was 20%. Women without a diploma saw an unemployment rate of less than 5% (Haut Commissariat au Plan, *Enquête nationale sur l'emploi*). In Egypt in 2012, women with a secondary education had the

highest unemployment rate (76%), followed by those with a tertiary education (47%), primary education (17%) or less (6%).

8. In Jordan, men are 3.4 times more likely to be engaged in early-stage entrepreneurial activity. In Morocco, the TEA rate is 6.1% for men and 2.9% for women. In Tunisia, the TEA is 15% for males and 5.3% for females. In Algeria, where men are almost twice as likely to start a business as women, the TEA is 6.4% for males and 3.3% for females. In Libya, the TEA is 14.8% for men and 7.2% for women.

9. "Necessity" refers to a "lack of alternative opportunities for earning income", whereas "opportunity" is characterised by "belief in the existence of profitable opportunities in the market" (OECD, 2014:60).

10. According to World Bank Enterprise Surveys, "Female participation in ownership" refers to the presence of at least one woman among the principal owners of the business.

11. While the value in Algeria is also low, it is from 2007 and thus cannot be easily compared with that of Tunisia from 2013.

12. Unweighted average for 12 OECD countries (World Bank Enterprise Surveys).

References

Ahmed, W.M. (2012), "Gender pay gap in Egypt", *Working Paper*, No. 14, Economic Commission for Europe, Conference of European Statisticians, www.unece.org:8080/fileadmin/DAM/stats/documents/ece/ces/ge.30/2012/14_EGY_E.pdf.

Assaad, R. (2014), "Making sense of Arab labor markets: The enduring legacy of dualism, *IZA Journal of Labor & Development*, Vol. 3/1, http://ftp.iza.org/dp7573.pdf.

Assaad, R., and M. Arntz (2005), "Constrained geographical mobility and gendered labor market outcomes under structural adjustment: Evidence from Egypt, *World Development*, Vol. 33/3, pp. 431-454, http://dx.doi.org/10.1016/j.worlddev.2004.08.007.

Assaad, R., and G. Barsoum (2007), "Youth exclusion in Egypt: In search of "second chances", *Middle East Youth Initiative Working Paper*, No. 2, World Bank, Washington, DC, http://datatopics.worldbank.org/hnp/files/edstats/EGYpub07.pdf.

Assaad, R., R. Hendy and C. Yassine (2012), "Gender and the Jordanian labor market", in *The Jordanian Labour Market in the New Millennium* (Ed. Ragui Assaad), Oxford University Press, Oxford, http://archive.hhh.umn.edu/people/rassaad/pdf/Gender_in_Jordan.pdf.

Barro, R.J. and J.W. Lee (2013), "Barro-Lee dataset of Educational Attainment" (dataset), www.barrolee.com.

Berniell, M. and C. Sánchez-Páramo (2012), "Overview of time use data used for the analysis of gender differences in time use patterns", *World Development Report Background Paper.*

Biltagy, M. (2014), "Estimation of gender wage differentials in Egypt using Oaxaca Decomposition Technique. *Topics in Middle Eastern and North African Economies*, Vol. 16/1, pp. 17-42, www.luc.edu/orgs/meea/volume16/pdfs/Biltagy.pdf.

CAPMAS (2014), *Annual Bulletin of the Statistics of Employment, Wages And Working Hours*, Egyptian Central Agency for Public Mobilization and Statistics, www.capmas.gov.eg/.

Chamlou, N. (2008), *The Environment for Women's Entrepreneurship in the Middle East and North Africa*, World Bank, Washington, DC, http://siteresources.worldbank.org/INTMENA/Resources/Environment_for_Womens_Entrepreneurship_in_MNA_final.pdf.

Dhillon, N. et al. (2009), *Missed by the Boom, Hurt by the Bust: Making Markets Work for Young People in the Middle East*, Middle East Youth Initiative, Washington, DC, https://www.brookings.edu/wp-content/uploads/2016/06/05_middle_east_youth_dhillon_final.pdf.

EFE, Bayt.com and YouGov (2015), *First Jobs for Young Women in the Middle East & North Africa: Expectations And Reality*, Education For Employment, https://www.slideshare.net/bayt_com/first-jobs-for-young-women-in-the-middle-east-and-north-africa-white-paper.

Elgazzar, H. et al. (2015), *Labor Market Dynamics In Libya: Reintegration For Recovery*, World Bank Study, Washington, DC, https://openknowledge.worldbank.org/handle/10986/22015.

European Training Foundation (2014), *Young People Not in Employment, Education or Training in the ETF Partner Countries*, European Communities Luxembourg, https://www.etf.europa.eu/webatt.nsf/0/A0A1BB4102618130C1257E3000329DCA/$file/Young%20people%20not%20in%20employment,%20education%20or%20training%20in%20the%20ETF%20partner%20countries.pdf.

Ferrant, G. and A. Kolev (2016), "The economic cost of gender-based discrimination in social institutions", *OECD Development Centre Issues Paper*, OECD, Paris, www.oecd.org/dev/development-gender/SIGI_cost_final.pdf.

Galal, A. (2002), *The Paradox of Education and Unemployment in Egypt*, Egyptian Centre for Economic Studies, Cairo, http://citeseerx.ist.psu.edu/viewdoc/download?doi=10.1.1.128.640&rep=rep1&type=pdf.

GEM (2015), *Adult Population Survey Measures, 2015*, Global Entrepreneurship Monitor, London, www.gemconsortium.org/data.

GEM (2013), *Global Entrepreneurship Monitor 2012 Women's Report*, Global Entrepreneurship Monitor, London, www.babson.edu/Academics/centers/blank-center/global-research/gem/Documents/GEM%202012%20Womens%20Report.pdf.

GEM (Global Entrepreneurship Monitor) national and global reports are accessible at http://gemconsortium.org.

High Commission of Planning (2013), "High Commission of Planning, Morocco Dataset 2013", Morocco, www.hcp.ma.

Houriet-Segard, G. and J.M. Pasteels (2011), *Projections of Economically Active Population: A Review of National and International Methodologies*, International Labour Office, Geneva, www.ilo.org/wcmsp5/groups/public/---dgreports/---stat/documents/publication/wcms_213755.pdf.

ILO (2016), "ILOSTAT Database: ILO Database Of Labour Statistics", International Labour Organization, Geneva.

ILO (2015a), *Women in Business and Management: Gaining Momentum*, International Labour Office, Geneva, www.ilo.org/wcmsp5/groups/public/---dgreports/---dcomm/---publ/documents/publication/wcms_316450.pdf.

ILO (2015b), *Global Employment Trends for Youth 2015: Scaling Up Investments in Decent Jobs for Youth*, International Labour Office, Geneva, www.ilo.org/wcmsp5/groups/public/---dgreports/---dcomm/---publ/documents/publication/wcms_412015.pdf.

Monitor, G.E. (2010), *GEM-MENA Regional Report 2009*, International Development Research Centre, Cairo.

Mryyan, N. (2014), "Demographics, labor force participation and unemployment In Jordan", *Economic Research Forum Working Paper*, No. 670, Giza, Egypt, https://erf.org.eg/wp-content/uploads/2014/08/670.pdf.

Ñopo, H., N. Daza and J. Ramos (2011), "Gender earnings gaps in the world", *IZA Discussion Paper*, No. 5736, Bonn, http://ftp.iza.org/dp5736.pdf.

OECD (2015), *In It Together: Why Less Inequality Benefits All*, OECD Publishing, Paris, http://dx.doi.org/10.1787/9789264235120-en.

OECD (2014a), *Women in Business 2014: Accelerating Entrepreneurship in the Middle East and North Africa Region*, OECD Publishing, Paris, http://dx.doi.org/10.1787/9789264213944-en.

OECD (2014b), *Women in Public Life: Gender, Law and Policy in the Middle East and North Africa*, OECD Publishing, Paris, http://dx.doi.org/10.1787/9789264224636-en.

OECD (2012), *Women in Business: Policies to Support Women's Entrepreneurship Development in the MENA Region*, OECD Publishing, Paris, http://dx.doi.org/10.1787/9789264179073-en.

OECD/IDRC (2013), *New Entrepreneurs and High Performance Enterprises in the Middle East and North Africa*, OECD Publishing, Paris, http://dx.doi.org/10.1787/9789264179196-en.

Sabha, Y. (18 April 2014), "Youth employment in Egypt and Tunisia vs. Jordan and Morocco three years after the Arab awakening", *World Bank blog*, http://blogs.worldbank.org/arabvoices/youth-employment-egypt-and-tunisia-vs-jordan-and-morocco-three-years-after-arab-awakening.

Sayre, E., and R. Hendy (2013), "Female labor supply in Egypt, Tunisia, and Jordan", *Paper presented at the ASSA Meetings in Philadelphia* (accessed on 18 June 2015).

Sekkat, K., A. Szafarz and I. Tojerow (2015), "Women at the top in developing countries: Evidence from firm-level data, *IZA Discussion Paper*, No. 9537, Bonn, http://ftp.iza.org/dp9537.pdf.

Stampini, M. and A. Verdier-Chouchane (2011) "Labor market dynamics in Tunisia: The issue of youth unemployment", *Review of Middle-East Economics and Finance*, Vol. 7, No. 2, September 2011, pp. 1-35, African Development Bank, Tunis, www.afdb.org/fileadmin/uploads/afdb/Documents/Publications/Working%20Paper%20%20No%20123%20%20PDF%20%20.pdf.

Sweidan, M. (2012), "Male-female pay differences, Jordanian case", *UNECE Working Paper*, No. 23, Conference on European Statisticians, Economic Commission for Europe, Geneva, 12-14 March 2012, http://unstats.un.org/unsd/gender/Mexico_Nov2014/Session%202%20Jordan.pdf.

Tijdens, K., and M. Klaveren (2012), "Frozen in time: Gender pay gap unchanged for 10 years", *ITUC Report*, Brussels, www.ituc-csi.org/frozen-in-time-gender-pay-gap.html.

Tunisian National Institute of Statistics (2015), National Institute of Statistics (database), Tunisia, http://beta.ins.tn/en/themes/emploi#sub-374.

UIS (2016), UNESCO Institute of Statistics (database), UIS, Montreal, http://data.uis.unesco.org/.

UNESCO (2012), "Youth and skills: Putting education to work", *Education for All Global Monitoring Report*, UNESCO, Paris, http://unesdoc.unesco.org/images/0021/002180/218003e.pdf.

World Bank (2016), Enterprise Survey (database), Washington, DC, www.enterprisesurveys.org/data.

World Bank (2016), Gender Statistics (database), Washington, DC, http://databank.worldbank.org/data/reports.aspx?source=Gender%20Statistics.

World Bank (2016), World Bank Development Indicators (database), Washington, DC, http://databank.worldbank.org/data/reports.aspx?source=world-development-indicators.

World Bank (2014), "Arab Republic of Egypt – More jobs, better jobs: A priority for Egypt", *World Bank Study*, World Bank Group, Washington, DC, http://documents.worldbank.org/curated/en/926831468247461895/Arab-Republic-of-Egypt-More-jobs-better-jobs-a-priority-for-Egypt.

World Bank (2007), *The Status & Progress of Women in the Middle East & North Africa*, World Bank, Washington, DC, http://siteresources.worldbank.org/INTMENA/Resources/MENA_Gender_Compendium-2009-1.pdf.

World Bank/International Finance Corporation (2013), *Women, Business and the Law 2014: Removing Restrictions to Enhance Gender Equality,* World Bank/International Finance Corporation, Washington, DC, http://wbl.worldbank.org/~/media/WBG/WBL/Documents/Reports/2014/Women-Business-and-the-Law-2014-FullReport.pdf?la=en.

Chapter 2

International and constitutional commitments and women's access to justice in selected MENA countries

This chapter presents the legal framework for women's empowerment established by international conventions and regional commitments, in particular the principle of equality and the right to work. It reviews the valuable efforts of all six countries to grant women and men equal rights in line with international commitments. It also notes that effective implementation of constitutional commitments requires that they be incorporated at other legislative levels and underpinned by effective enforcement mechanisms through the justice system. The chapter describes how women in the six countries can gain access to courts via international conventions, national constitutions, labour and business laws, and family law. It presents suggestions for increasing women's awareness of their legal rights and improving their access to justice.

Introduction

The law provides a starting point for social change. The ability of women to enjoy their legal rights is both empowering and a prerequisite for building inclusive and prosperous societies. Legal amendments may work as a vehicle of evolution in social behaviour, and social change may in turn generate changes in the law. For reforms to take root and bear fruit, however, aspirational legal commitments to equality must permeate national laws and eventually evolve into social norms. States that commit to international conventions and principles establishing general standards must incorporate them through their constitutions and amendments to domestic legislation.

Algeria, Egypt, Jordan, Libya, Morocco and Tunisia are signatories to key international conventions that commit governments to furthering gender equality and non-discrimination between women and men. They are also committed to regional standards on gender equality and non-discrimination.

Five of the six countries – Algeria, Egypt, Jordan, Morocco and Tunisia – have adopted new constitutions over the past several years with provisions that strengthen the status of women. In Libya, the ratification of a permanent constitution is expected to replace the provisional Constitutional Declaration, in place since August 2011. These new charters were enacted following citizens' calls throughout the region for greater democracy, better governance and reduced inequalities. They guarantee gender equality and set the basis for a more balanced involvement of women in their countries' economies. Nevertheless, governments may engage in further efforts to align with international instruments and work towards equal access to economic opportunities for women and men.

Access to justice is also essential to reduce gender-based discrimination. Empowering women to claim their rights is central to both legal protection and the enforcement of gender-equality provisions. Respect of rights can be guaranteed only through effective remedies and adequate reparation in cases of failure to apply the law. Judicial decisions that redress a wrong pave the way for society to adapt to changes towards women and for women themselves to use those decisions in their professional and personal lives.

In principle, women in the six countries under review have access to courts to ensure the enforcement of international, constitutional and national legislative provisions. In practice, however, their rights are inhibited by a number of hurdles: the courts do not always enforce the rules, the judiciary may lack knowledge of current principles and standards, women are often not aware of their rights and, even when they are, social norms and financial constraints may hinder them from going to court. The fact that few judges are women may also be a factor.

Role of international conventions in guaranteeing gender equality

Several instruments have established general international standards on gender equality and non-discrimination, as well as the right to work.

The 1948 Universal Declaration of Human Rights (UDHR)[1] and the two 1966 United Nations Covenants, on Civil and Political Rights (ICCPR) and on Economic, Social and Cultural Rights (ICESCR), apply to women and men, ensuring the general principles of freedom and equality. The six countries have ratified the two covenants (Algeria 1989, Egypt 1982, Jordan 1975, Libya 1970, Morocco 1979 and Tunisia 1969).

Box 2.1. Equality and the right to work in the 1966 UN covenants

Article 3 of both the ICCPR and the ICESCR (on equality)

The States Parties to the Covenant undertake to ensure the equal right of men and women to the enjoyment of all civil and political rights set forth in the Covenant.

Article 26 of the ICCPR (on equality)

All persons are equal before the law and are entitled without any discrimination to the equal protection of the law. In this respect, the law shall prohibit any discrimination and guarantee to all persons equal and effective protection against discrimination on any ground such as race, colour, sex, language, religion, political or other opinion, national or social origin, property, birth or other status.

Article 3 of the ICESCR (on equality)

The States Parties to the present Covenant undertake to ensure the equal right of men and women to the enjoyment of all economic, social and cultural rights set forth in the present Covenant.

Article 6 of the ICESCR (on work)

1. The States Parties to the present Covenant recognize the right to work, which includes the right of everyone to the opportunity to gain his living by work which he freely chooses or accepts, and will take appropriate steps to safeguard this right.
2. The steps to be taken by a State Party to the present Covenant to achieve the full realisation of this right shall include technical and vocational guidance and training programmes, policies and techniques to achieve steady economic, social and cultural development and full and productive employment under conditions safeguarding fundamental political and economic freedoms to the individual."

Article 7 of the ICESCR (on work)

The States Parties to the present Covenant recognize the right of everyone to the enjoyment of just and favourable conditions of work which ensure, in particular:

(a) Remuneration which provides all workers, as a minimum, with:

  (i) Fair wages and equal remuneration for work of equal value without distinction of any kind, in particular women being guaranteed conditions of work not inferior to those enjoyed by men, with equal pay for equal work;

  (ii) provisions of the present Covenant;

(b) Safe and healthy working conditions;

(c) Equal opportunity for everyone to be promoted in his employment to an appropriate higher level, subject to no considerations other than those of seniority and competence.

Source: UN General Assembly, International Covenant on Civil and Political Rights, 16 December 1966, United Nations, Treaty Series, Vol. 999, p. 171, www.refworld.org/docid/3ae6b3aa0.html; UN General Assembly, International Covenant on Economic, Social and Cultural Rights, 16 December 1966, United Nations, Treaty Series, Vol. 993, p. 3, www.refworld.org/docid/3ae6b36c0.html.

In addition to these general human rights principles, the six states have ratified and are committed to standards set by international conventions that specifically target eliminating gender-based discrimination and realising gender equality. The UN Convention on the Elimination of All Forms of Discrimination against Women (CEDAW) is a landmark agreement covering a wide spectrum of human rights. It also refers to several ILO conventions that specifically regard international standards affecting women's employment. Finally, the countries analysed have also made pledges to non-binding recommendations on gender equality and women's economic integration.

The next sections will review key elements of these conventions and take a closer look at the constitutional provisions relating to gender equality in the six countries.

The UN Convention on the Elimination of All Forms of Discrimination against Women

CEDAW was adopted by the UN General Assembly in 1979. Article 1 defines discrimination against women as "any distinction, exclusion or restriction made on the basis of sex which has the effect or purpose of impairing or nullifying the recognition, enjoyment or exercise by women, irrespective of their marital status, on a basis of equality of men and women, of human rights and fundamental freedoms in the political, economic, social, cultural, civil or any other field."

As of January 2016, 189 states had ratified CEDAW, committing to adopt all appropriate measures to ensure that the rights affirmed in the text are exercised in full. Every four years, the countries must submit a report outlining the measures taken in compliance with their treaty obligations to the Committee on the Elimination of Discrimination against Women, an independent committee of experts that addresses recommendations to the concerned states.

The Optional Protocol to CEDAW, a side agreement adopted by the General Assembly in 1999 that entered into force in 2000, allows the Committee on the Elimination of Discrimination against Women to consider complaints from individuals and groups that fall within their jurisdiction. As of January 2016, 106 states were parties to the Protocol, including Libya (2004), Tunisia (2008) and Morocco (2016).

Reservations to CEDAW

When ratifying CEDAW, all six states introduced reservations, which exclude or modify the legal effect of certain provisions. CEDAW allows states to enter reservations at the time of signature, ratification or accession to the treaty, on the condition that the reservations are not "incompatible with the object and purpose of the present Convention" (Article 28, paragraph 2).

Of the six countries under review, all except Jordan introduced general declarations or reservations regarding Article 2, which requires that all interested states apply the convention at the national level and take all necessary measures to prevent discrimination against women.[2] These reservations, according to which the states will apply Article 2 provided it does not conflict with provisions of Islamic Sharia law, were considered in conflict with the object and purpose of the convention by the CEDAW Committee[3] and by a number of other States Parties (Freeman, 2009).[4] These objections, however, are more political than legal in their impact and thus do not prevent the convention's entry into force.

Table 2.1. **Status of ratification and reservations to CEDAW**

	Algeria	Egypt	Jordan	Libya	Morocco	Tunisia
Ratification	1996	1981	1992	1989	1993	1985
Optional Protocol				2004	2016	2008
Reservations to Art. 2 (application of the convention / general declaration)	Yes[1]	Yes[2]	No	Yes[3]	Yes[4]	Yes[5]
Reservations to Art. 9 (rights to nationality)	Yes (removed in 2008)	Yes (removed in 2008)	Yes (article 9 para. 2)	No	Yes (removed in 2011)	Yes (removed in 2014)
Reservations to Art. 15 (women's equality with men and legal capacity)	Yes (para. 4 on freedom of movement)	No	Yes (removed in 2009)	No	Yes (para. 4 on freedom of movement)	Yes (removed in 2014)
Reservations to Art. 16 (marriage, family relations)	Yes	Yes	Yes, para 1(c) (d)(g)[6]	Yes, para 1(c) and (d)[7]	Yes (removed in 2011)	Yes (removed in 2014)

Source: Author's own research based on CEDAW.

Notes:

1. "The government of the People's Democratic Republic of Algeria declares itself willing to apply the provisions of this article providing that they are not in conflict with the provisions of the Algerian family code."
2. "Reservation to all of the provisions of Article 2, the sub-paragraphs of which the Arab Republic of Egypt is willing to apply providing that these are not in conflict with the provisions set forth in the Muslim Sharia."
3. "In order for Article 2 of the Convention to be applied, it is necessary to take duly into account the peremptory norms decreed by the Islamic Sharia with regard to determining the share of inheritance of a deceased person to which each male or female heir has a right."
4. "1. Regarding Article 2: The government of the Kingdom of Morocco declares that it is willing to apply the provisions of this article, provided that:
   – they have no impact on the constitutional provisions regulating succession to the throne in Morocco;
   – they are not in conflict with the provisions set forth in the Islamic Sharia, given that certain provisions contained within the Moroccan code of personal status (granting a woman different rights from those granted to her husband) cannot be transgressed or revoked due to the fact that they are essentially borrowed from the Islamic Sharia, one of the aims of which is to ensure a balance between man and wife in order to maintain strong family ties."
5. "The Tunisian government declares that it shall not adopt any administrative or legislative decision by virtue of the convention if it is likely to go against the first chapter of the Tunisian Constitution."
6. 1(c): same rights and responsibilities during marriage and at its dissolution; (d): same rights and responsibilities as parents irrespective of their marital status, (g): same personal rights as husband and wife, including the right to choose a family name, a profession and an occupation.
7. See previous note.

Algeria, Egypt, Libya, Morocco and Tunisia originally introduced reservations to Article 16, which guarantees equality between men and women in all matters relating to marriage and family relations, including the rights of equal ownership, acquisition, management and administration as well as disposition of property by both spouses. These reservations have since been lifted by Morocco (2011) and Tunisia (2014). Of the reservations still standing, Algeria's indicates that the article "shall not contradict the provisions of the Family Code", Egypt's that it "shall not prejudice the Islamic Sharia's provisions whereby women are accorded rights equivalent to those of their spouses so as to ensure a just balance between them", and Libya's that it "shall not contradict any of the rights guaranteed to women by the Islamic Sharia".

Algeria, Egypt, Morocco and Tunisia have lifted their reservations to Article 9 (equal rights between men and women with respect to the nationality of their children). Only Jordan has maintained its reservation, while Libya did not enter a reservation on that article.

On provisions central to women's economic empowerment and participation, reservations have been introduced but are not systematic, and some have been lifted. None of the six countries made reservations on Article 11, which guarantees non-discrimination against women in employment and labour-standard requirements such as the right to work, the right to the same employment opportunities, the right to equal remuneration, the right to social security and the protection of pregnancy and maternity (see Chapter 3). There are no remaining reservations to Article 15 paragraph 2, which covers the right to conclude contracts and administer property. Algeria and Morocco introduced reservations, however, on the movement of persons and the freedom to choose their domicile, which is addressed in Article 15 paragraph 4. Reservations on the same paragraph have been lifted by Jordan (2009) and Tunisia (2014).

By withdrawing reservations, countries signal progress on women's empowerment and show their closer compliance with the spirit of the convention. Nevertheless, real progress depends on effective implementation at the domestic level.

Implementation of CEDAW at the national level

Both the method, by which treaties become domestic law, and the status they enjoy in national legal systems, depend on the constitutional law of the ratifying state. To meet their CEDAW commitments, states that are parties to the convention must repeal or amend inconsistent domestic law provisions and adopt measures ensuring that individuals subject to their jurisdiction enjoy the relevant rights. The CEDAW Committee has emphasised that States Parties must ensure that "through constitutional amendments or by other appropriate legislative means, the principle of equality between women and men and of non-discrimination is enshrined in domestic law with an overriding and enforceable status. […] States Parties have an obligation to take steps to modify or abolish existing laws, regulations, customs and practices which constitute discrimination against women." (CEDAW, 2010a).

The CEDAW Committee acknowledges that the convention has had an important impact on legislative developments, institutional frameworks and policies towards women's rights in the six countries over the last 30 years. It has highlighted some examples in its examination of the country reports:

- **Algeria** created a Ministry for the Family and the Status of Women (CEDAW 2003) and established a National Council on the Family and Women (CEDAW, 2010b).
- **Egypt** established an Ombudsman Office in 2001 to receive and monitor women's complaints (CEDAW, 2008).
- **Morocco** pursued a national strategy for gender equity and equality by integrating a gender approach into all development policies and programmes (CEDAW, 2007a), as well as gender-sensitive budgeting (CEDAW, 2007b).
- **Jordan** amended its legislation to eliminate discrimination against women, including the Income Tax Act, the Penal Code, the Civil Status Act and the Personal Status Act (CEDAW, 2006).

- **Tunisia** reviewed discriminatory laws in the Code of Personal Status and the Nationality Code and took several legislative initiatives to address women's and girls' social protection (CEDAW, 2010c).

A more detailed analysis of constitutional gender-related provisions, as well as other legal provisions on women's economic empowerment, will be made in subsequent sections, with updates on progress made since CEDAW ratification.

Labour standards in the ILO conventions

Women's and men's employment and economic participation are also affected by other international provisions, in particular international labour standards for the protection of workers and for gender equality in the workplace. The ILO establishes such standards through international conventions and recommendations.

The six countries have ratified some conventions that protect employees from gender discrimination (Table 2.2). Only some ILO provisions specifically target improving the economic status of women: the elimination of sex-based discrimination in employment, the balance of work and family responsibilities, and the protection of maternity rights. Reservations to ILO conventions are not admissible under the standard-setting procedure (tripartite: government representatives, employers and workers' organisations) (UN, 2007).

The ILO standards are to be incorporated into States Parties' labour laws. States Parties commit to apply the provisions of these conventions and to submit periodic reports to the ILO Committee of Experts on the Application of Conventions and Recommendations (CEACR) on their implementation measures. Every two or five years, depending on the convention, the states must submit reports detailing the steps they have taken in law and practice to apply the conventions. Copies of their reports are submitted to employers' and workers' organisations, who may comment on them.[5] The committee of experts meets annually to review the reports on governments' compliance with the conventions and prepares observations that are published in its annual report, which is then examined and discussed during the ILO's annual assembly. The committee can also make direct requests that relate to more technical questions or ask for further information. The requests are not published in the report but are communicated directly to the governments concerned.

Specific observations by country include:

- **Algeria**: In 2014, the committee welcomed the adoption by Algeria of a number of measures aimed at improving the status of women and increasing their participation in managerial and decision-making posts, in particular the strengthening of employment support programmes for women (creation of micro-enterprises, microcredit, social integration of graduates, neighbourhood projects in rural areas, etc.). However, the committee noted that the economic activity rate for women remains particularly low and that it is changing slowly despite the high rate of school enrolment for girls and the significant proportion of women graduates. The committee encouraged the government to intensify its efforts to promote women's employment at all levels, particularly in the private sector, and throughout the country, including in rural areas. It asked the government to adopt practical measures against gender bias and stereotypes relating to women's aspirations and capabilities and their suitability for certain jobs; to enable male and female workers to reconcile work and family responsibilities; and to supply information on the impact of these measures, including statistics on the situation of men and women in employment in both the public and private sectors.[6]

Table 2.2. **Status of ratification of ILO conventions with gender relevance**

	Algeria	Egypt	Jordan	Libya	Morocco	Tunisia
Equal Remuneration Convention, 1951[1]	1962	1960	1966	1962	1979	1968
Social Security (Minimum Standards) Convention, 1952[2]	1969	No	2014 *(has accepted parts V, VI, IX, X)*[3]	1975 *(has accepted parts II to X)*[4]	No	No
Discrimination (Employment and Occupation) Convention, 1958[5]	1969	1960	1963	1961	1963	1959
Equality of Treatment (Social Security) Convention, 1962[6]	No	1993 *(has accepted branches a. to h.)*[7]	1963 *(has accepted branches c.d.f.g.)*[8]	1975 *(has accepted branches a. to i.)*[9]	No	1965 *(has accepted branches a. to g. and i.)*[10]
Workers with Family Responsibilities Convention, 1981[11]	No	No	No	No	No	No
Occupational Health Services Convention, 1985[12]	No	No	No	No	No	No
Maternity Protection Convention, 2000[13]	No	No	No	No	2011	No
1948 Night Work Convention[14]	1962	1960	No	1962	No	1957
Protocol of 1990 to the Night Work (Women) Convention (Revised), 1948[15]	No	No	No	No	No	2000

Source: Author's research work based on NORMLEX Information System on International Labour Standards, www.ilo.org/dyn/normlex/en/f?p=1000:11001:::NO:::.

Notes:

1. The Convention entered into force in 1953 and has been ratified by 171 member states. It applies to all workers in all economic sectors, private or public.
2. The Convention concerning Minimum Standards of Social Security entered into force in 1955 and has been ratified by 52 member states.
3. Part V: Old-age benefits, part VI: Employment injury benefits, part IX: Invalidity benefit, part X: Survivors' benefit.
4. Part II: Medical care, part III: Sickness benefit, part IV: Unemployment benefit, part V: Old-age benefit, part VI: Employment injury benefit, part VII: Family benefit, part VIII: Maternity benefit, part IX: Invalidity benefit, part X: Survivors' benefit.
5. This Convention concerning Discrimination in Respect of Employment and Occupation entered into force in 1960 and as of January 2016 has been ratified by 171 member states. It applies to all workers in all sectors of activity see NORMLEX, Information System on International Labour Standards, www.ilo.org/normlex.
6. The Convention concerning Equality of Treatment of Nationals and Non-Nationals in Social Security entered into force in 1964 and as of January 2016 has been ratified by 38 member states.
7. All branches of social security except family benefit.
8. c: maternity benefits, d: invalidity benefit, f: survivors' benefit, g: employment injury benefit.
9. All branches of social security.
10. All branches of social security except unemployment benefit.
11. The Convention concerning Workers with Family Responsibilities entered into force in 1983 and as of January 2016 has been ratified by 44 member states.
12. The Convention concerning Occupational Health Services entered into force in 1988 and as of January 2016 has been ratified by 32 member states.
13. This convention entered into force in 2002. It revised the Maternity Protection Convention of 1952 that was providing for 12 weeks and as of January 2016 had only been ratified by Libya (1975) from the 6 states concerned. The convention applies to all women in all employment relationships.
14. The Convention concerning Night Work of Women Employed in Industry entered into force in 1951 and as of January 2016 has been ratified by 67 member states.
15. The Protocol of 1990 to the Convention concerning Night Work of Women Employed in Industry entered into force in 1990 and as of January 2016 has been ratified by 3 countries.

- **Morocco**: In 2014, the committee noted with interest Morocco's adoption of Ikram, a four-year government plan for gender equality (2012-16) that has a significant budget, lays out 143 measures and sets 24 goals in eight areas. The Committee noted that the state budget had included a gender component since 2005 to take account of the differentiated concerns of women, men, girls and boys, and that a report on the gender budget, which now covers 27 ministerial departments, had been drafted and submitted to parliament each year. The committee also noted that, according to the government, the National Agency for the Promotion of Small and Medium-Sized Enterprises (ANPME) has implemented a number of programmes to promote women's access to entrepreneurship and to address the difficulties women confront when setting up their enterprises (limited access to credit, training and information). While stressing the government's continuous efforts to make equality between men and women a central component of its policy and the progress achieved in this area, the committee requested that the government provide information on specific measures taken, in the context of Ikram, to combat discrimination against women and promote equality between men and women in employment and occupation, and on the outcomes achieved in women's access to employment in the private and public sectors, the diversification of employment opportunities and training, and the improvement of working conditions.[7]
- **Egypt**: In 2012, the committee emphasised that the equal-remuneration provisions of Egypt's Labour Law of 2003 did not fully reflect the principle of equal remuneration for men and women for work of equal value as set forth in the convention. The committee therefore urged the government to take appropriate measures to amend the law in order to provide for equal remuneration for men and women for equal, the same or similar work, and to address situations where men and women perform different jobs, using different skills and involving different working conditions, but that are nevertheless jobs of equal value.[8]
- **Jordan**: In 2013, the committee noted the absence of legislative provisions clearly defining and prohibiting direct and indirect discrimination, covering all aspects of employment and occupation, including recruitment. It also noted insufficient protection against sexual harassment in employment and occupation. The committee noted as well that women are excluded from working in a range of industries and occupations, and that restrictions apply to work at night. The committee considered these broad limitations on women's employment as constituting obstacles to the recruitment and employment of women and as contrary to the principle of equality of opportunity and treatment of men and women in employment and occupation. It recalled that protective measures for women should be limited to the protection of maternity in the strictest sense, and that provisions relating to the protection of persons working under hazardous or difficult conditions should be aimed at protecting the health and safety of both men and women at work while taking account of gender differences with regard to specific risks to their health.[9]
- **Libya**: In 2008, the committee expressed serious concern about the persistent lack of information in the Libyan government's report on its obligation to declare and implement a national policy on equality with respect to all the grounds covered by the convention. It urged the government to provide full information on different aspects of equality of opportunity and treatment of men and women with respect to employment and occupation, vocational training and placement services in order to allow it to assess to what extent real progress has been made on the promotion of women's participation in all fields and on a wide range of job opportunities at all levels.[10]

- **Tunisia**: In 2014, the committee welcomed the adoption of the new Tunisian Constitution but reminded the government that constitutional provisions are not sufficient to ensure the full application of ILO conventions. Similarly, the fact that the authorities have not received any complaints does not mean that there is no discrimination but may rather indicate that the victims of discrimination have inadequate knowledge of the relevant legal provisions and dispute-resolution procedures or fear possible reprisals by the employer. The committee requested that the government take measures to raise awareness among the public and social partners of the principles set out in the convention and of the legal provisions relating to equality of opportunity and treatment in employment and occupation. It also asked Tunisia to take measures to evaluate the effectiveness of dispute-resolution procedures, including any difficulties of a practical nature that male or female workers may encounter in obtaining legal redress for discrimination based on any of the grounds set out in the convention.[11]

The incorporation of ILO standards into the respective laws of the six countries will be further discussed in Chapter 4.

Other provisions on women's economic empowerment

In addition to adhering to binding conventions, governments of the MENA economies have expressed their commitment to women's empowerment by committing to other, non-binding standards.

Participating ministers in the 2007 MENA-OECD Ministerial Meeting committed to the Declaration on Fostering Women's Entrepreneurship in the MENA Region and supported the creation of the OECD-MENA Women's Business Forum (WBF). To implement the declaration and to set a clear roadmap to economically empowering women, the 2009 MENA-OECD Women Business Leaders Summit endorsed an Action Plan on Fostering Women's Entrepreneurship and Employment in the MENA Region. The plan outlines four pillars for action: *i)* encourage women's entrepreneurship and employment by creating a business-enabling environment; *ii)* facilitate business registration and growth through enhanced access to finance, in particular for women-owned businesses; *iii)* improve economic policy through better gender-disaggregated statistics and indicators; and *iv)* facilitate participation in the WBF and ensure increased contacts among business networks. The WBF is a wide network of more than 700 stakeholders from governments, the private sector and civil society that serves as a platform for research and policy dialogue to improve networking, knowledge and access to information through analytical research and policy recommendations set out in various discussion papers and publications.

The 2013 OECD Recommendation on Gender Equality in Education, Employment and Entrepreneurship and the 2015 OECD Recommendation on Gender Equality in Public Life, adopted by the OECD Council, are non-binding instruments open to OECD members and non-members (Box 2.2). Their principles may serve as a framework for further guidance on areas of concern for women's participation in the economy.

Noteworthy pledges on women's empowerment include the Arab League's Cairo Declaration on gender equality and women's empowerment in the Arab region (February 2014), and the conclusions of the Union for the Mediterranean's third ministerial conference on strengthening the role of women in society (September 2013). Both texts call for a comprehensive approach in support of women's empowerment and gender equality through women's political and economic empowerment, social transformation and the end of violence against women and girls (Box 2.3).

Box 2.2. **The OECD Gender Initiative and key gender recommendations**

The OECD Gender Initiative, launched in 2010, examined existing barriers to gender equality in education, employment and entrepreneurship with the aim of strengthening the evidence base, improving policies and promoting gender equality in the economies of OECD. Available evidence, policy analysis and actionable policy messages were presented in the OECD's *Closing the Gender Gap: Act Now*, launched in December 2012 (OECD, 2012a), along with the OECD Gender Portal, which includes a range of benchmark indicators on education, employment and entrepreneurship for OECD and key partner countries.

Based on the findings and policy recommendations in *Closing the Gender Gap*, the OECD developed a Recommendation on Gender Equality in Education, Employment and Entrepreneurship (the OECD Gender Recommendation), which was adopted by all OECD countries at the OECD Ministerial Council meeting on 29 May 2013. Since then, Costa Rica, Kazakhstan, Latvia, Lithuania and the Russian Federation have adhered to the Gender Recommendation. It notably recommends that governments introduce legislation, policies, monitoring and campaigning in order to provide equal access to education, close the gender pay gap, promote family-friendly policies, foster participation of fathers in unpaid work, move towards a better gender balance in leadership positions and promote entrepreneurship among women. It also recommends that OECD members and key partners contribute to progress towards gender equality in developing countries by prioritising investments that promote women's economic empowerment in development co-operation programmes. The recommendation proposes that member countries further these objectives through co-operation with all relevant stakeholders by developing, promoting and exchanging policy principles, guidelines, and best practices, as well as by reinforcing the production of internationally comparable gender-sensitive data. The OECD Gender Recommendation calls for a progress report on gender issues to be submitted to the OECD Council no later than four years following its adoption, and regularly thereafter. (full text: www.oecd.org/gender/C-MIN(2013)5-ENG.pdf).

As a complement to the 2013 Gender Recommendation, the OECD Council adopted a Recommendation on Gender Equality in Public Life on 14 December 2015 (OECD, 2016). This new recommendation is geared towards the effective implementation of gender equality. It seeks to mainstream initiatives in public life and enhance women's equal access to public leadership opportunities such as in parliaments, the executive, the judiciary and public administrations (full text: http://dx.doi.org/10.1787/9789264252820-en).

Box 2.3. **The Arab League's commitment to women's empowerment**

The Women, Family and Childhood Department at the League of Arab States has developed a Strategic Plan for women's empowerment in the Arab region. It is in line with the 2030 Sustainable Development Agenda and the principles and pillars of the 2014 Cairo Declaration for women in the Arab region. Together, the Cairo Declaration and the Strategic Plan represent a comprehensive framework for promoting women's status in the Arab region. They reaffirm the principles of human rights treaties and regional and international commitments, and address the specific challenges of the Arab region.

Outcome 4 of the Cairo Declaration calls for an increase of 50% in women's economic and workforce participation and demands that women have access to services and benefits.

Outcome 5 demands that women benefit from social-protection policies and services, including health, education and legal benefits, to improve their quality of life.

The Cairo Declaration has a provision for reviewing laws and establishing mechanisms to promote gender equality. It also has a pillar on gender mainstreaming in planning and budgeting, including gender-disaggregated data.

In 2016 the League of Arab States launched "Khadija", a platform to promote women's economic empowerment and advocate for legal reforms in the region, in partnership with UN Women and with the support of the OECD.

Source: UN Women (2014), www.unwomen.org/~/media/headquarters/attachments/sections/csw/58/csw58-declaration-cairo-en%20pdf.ashx.

The UN's 2030 Agenda for Sustainable Development provides an ambitious roadmap for women's economic empowerment through its Sustainable Development Goals, including elements of SDG 1 (women's equal rights to economic resources) and SDG 8 (full and productive employment and decent work and equal pay for equal value). The Addis Ababa Action Agenda of the third international conference on financing for development also identified women's equal rights as an essential element for achieving sustainable development, along with opportunities for participation in leadership in the economy.

Governments are not obliged to reflect these non-binding standards in national legal frameworks. They are encouraged, however, to embrace the goals and to establish the necessary frameworks to support their implementation.

Gender equality in constitutional texts

Commitments to international standards and principles provide guidance for countries and may act as benchmarks for steps to be taken at the domestic level in support of gender equality. It is important to acknowledge the six countries' progress in various areas, as well as to consider the historical evolution of their respective legal systems (Box 2.4). Since the beginning of the 2011 uprisings in the region, efforts have been made towards reducing gender discrimination and supporting women's empowerment, demonstrating the will of the authorities to strengthen women's rights and liberties.

Box 2.4. **Relatively recent legal systems**

The legal systems of Algeria, Egypt, Jordan, Libya, Morocco and Tunisia were secularised in the late 19th or early 20th century on the basis of Western law. Civil law, penal law and labour law, in particular, are inspired by French law. Islam is referenced as the countries' religion in the constitutions, and even as the main source of legislation (Egypt), but only family law (marriage, divorce, inheritance) still draws its roots from Sharia principles in all six countries, and to different degrees. The six countries follow a dual judicial system with separate sets of courts for administrative and private law matters, depending on the parties involved in the litigation. Only Jordan still has religious courts for family matters.

New constitutions have been adopted in Morocco (2011), Tunisia (2014) and Egypt (2014). Jordan amended its fundamental text in 2011 and Algeria in 2016. Libya does not yet have a permanent constitution; the provisional Constitutional Declaration, adopted in 2011 to administer the transitional period, is still in force.[12] Although few women took part in the drafting processes,[13] all constitutional texts strengthen their status by guaranteeing gender equality and setting the basis for a more balanced involvement of women in the countries' economies.

The enhanced protection of women's rights at the constitutional level and their equal status with men can have a major impact on improving women's access to economic positions in the MENA countries. The constitutions of Algeria, Egypt, Jordan, Libya, Morocco and Tunisia are the supreme law of the country and have pre-eminence over all other national laws. This implies that, in principle, all six states are bound to repeal or amend inconsistent provisions in underlying domestic laws.

Equality and non-discrimination

The standards set by CEDAW and the ILO are also embedded in the constitutions of the six countries. The constitutions guarantee the principle of equality and prohibit discrimination, albeit under rather different terms (Annex 2.A1). These differences can have a significant influence on laws governing the status of women, particularly in the context of family law, and can affect women's access to economic activity.

The principle of equality between men and women has been integrated into the new constitutions of Morocco, Tunisia and Egypt for the first time.

- In **Morocco**, the constitution states that men and women are granted equal civil, political, economic, social, cultural and environmental rights and liberties included in the constitution and the international treaties ratified by Morocco (Article 19).[14] The state undertakes to realise parity between men and women and provides for the creation of an Authority for Parity and the Struggle against All Forms of Discrimination (Article 19). This authority should be consulted on projects relating to laws and public policies connected to women's rights. It should also be able to issue recommendations and implement initiatives to raise awareness of gender discrimination and to promote equal education.[15] Morocco is the only country to have a provision in its constitution to establish such an institution.
- In **Tunisia**, this equality is expressed in the most absolute terms: "Both male and female citizens are equal in terms of their rights and responsibilities. They are equal before the law without any discrimination" (Article 21).
- In **Egypt**, the state is committed to ensuring this equality "for all civil, political, economic, social and cultural rights" (Article 11), which could potentially exclude equality within the family since family rights are not mentioned.

Discrimination based on gender is also prohibited in the constitutions of Algeria, Jordan and Libya.

- In **Algeria**, the constitution declares the principle of equality among all citizens and specifically prohibits discrimination based on gender (Article 32). It adds that institutions shall aim to ensure equality of rights and responsibilities for all citizens, whether male or female, by removing obstacles that hinder the development of the individual and prevent the effective participation of all in political, economic, social and cultural life (Article 34).
- In **Jordan**, the constitution states the principle of equality and prohibits discrimination on the grounds of race, language and religion but does not include gender (Article 6). In 2011, civil society organisations attempted in vain to introduce this specification.
- The provisional constitutional declaration in **Libya** also forbids discrimination, without specifically applying the prohibition to gender-based discrimination.

Despite the declaration of the principle of equality on the constitutional and international levels, some nationality laws allow forms of discrimination among citizens. Although several countries have recently amended their nationality laws (Morocco, Egypt, Algeria and Tunisia), others (Jordan and Libya) continue to prohibit mothers from transmitting their nationality to their children. In Egypt, the constitution of 2014 expressly sanctions a principle already laid down in the nationality law in 2004 that allows both the father and the mother to pass nationality to their children. However, although an Egyptian husband may transmit his nationality to his foreign spouse (acquisition of nationality by marriage), an Egyptian wife who marries a foreigner is not entitled to transmit her nationality to her spouse. The same is true in Morocco.

Economic and political participation

One of the key elements of gender equality is women's ability to participate in economic activities, whether in the private or the public sector. Women's participation in political life is important both in itself and for the change it can bring to societies at large. An essential prerequisite for women's economic activity is that they be granted access to the labour force, and the six constitutions provide that all citizens have the right to work (Annex 2.A2).

Certain recent constitutional provisions require the state to grant women access to specific professional situations, in particular those with higher responsibility:

- **Egypt** is committed to encouraging women to access high positions in the public and legal sectors (Article 11).
- **Tunisia** guarantees men and women equal opportunities to access all levels of responsibility in any field (Article 46). It also establishes, for the first time, the principle of women's eligibility for the presidency of the republic (Article 74).
- **Algeria's** 2016 amendment to the constitution declares that the state works to promote parity between men and women in the labour market and encourages the advancement of women's responsibilities in institutions, government and enterprises.

The presence of women in elected assemblies can have a positive impact on their participation in economic life, as female representatives may be more aware of women's economic issues and more likely to fight to implement measures to remedy inequalities. Women can also serve as role models and help to change attitudes, fostering a more constructive image of the role of women in society and within the state. Article 4 of CEDAW allows for temporary special measures to be taken, in appropriate circumstances, to accelerate achieving de facto equality of women with men. Algeria, Egypt, and Tunisia have recently adopted constitutional provisions encouraging the participation of women in political life.

- In **Algeria**, the state will work towards promoting women's political rights in order to increase their access to representation in elected assemblies (Article 35).
- In **Egypt**, the constitution of 2014 requires a 25% quota of female representation in local elections (Article 180) and "adequate" representation in parliament (Article 11). As a result, 56 of the parliament's 596 seats were reserved for women in the legislative elections of 2015.
- The **Tunisian** constitution declares that the state shall guarantee the representation of women in elected bodies (Article 34) and requires parity between women and men in elected councils (Article 46).

Fighting violence against women

Fighting violence against women is an important means of strengthening their status in society and their ability to integrate into economic life. Violence can be physical, sexual or psychological. It can take the form of threats or real acts, and it may occur in the public or the private sphere. In relation to economic activities, violence may impede women's ability to work by decreasing their performance on the job and impairing their productivity, leading to absenteeism or eventually their exclusion from the labour market.

The new Egyptian and Tunisian constitutions require, for the first time, that the state work actively to decrease violence towards women (Egypt, Article 11) and take the necessary measures to eradicate violence against women (Tunisia, Article 46).

Incorporation of constitutional provisions into national legal frameworks

Some constitutional provisions are so specific and detailed that they can be directly implemented. Individuals are able to claim these rights with no need for a specific law. In most cases, however, the provisions take the form of abstract declarations that set out general principles. Categorised as "non-self-executing", they cannot be invoked by individuals or applied by the courts until the legislature passes a law. This is the case for economic and social provisions, such as the right to work, that create positive claims against the state.

Many constitutional provisions are relatively new in Algeria, Egypt, Libya, Morocco and Tunisia, and legislators have not yet had an opportunity to incorporate the new principles into actual regulations. Because dynamic processes are involved, a certain amount of time may be required before reforms can be introduced into the legal framework and implemented.

In their efforts to implement constitutional guarantees and domestic laws, national parliaments may find themselves confronted with traditional societal models and stereotypes that can have a detrimental effect both on women's involvement in the economy and on domestic laws in relation to women's economic integration. As discussed in the next chapter, the implementation of legislative amendments in the six countries may also be affected by legal pluralism and rather complex layers of interpretation. These tensions and the resulting difficulties of interpretation are illustrated by the fact that different sets of constitutional provisions relate to human rights in public areas and to rights within the private sphere.

In the case of Egypt, the 2014 constitutional text says that the state shall ensure that women are able to "strike a balance between family duties and the demands of her work" (Article 11). This seems to imply that family duties are women's main responsibility, and it may thus contravene the equality principle of Article 9 of the constitution. In Jordan, the constitutional amendment of 2011 maintains that the family is the basis of society, "founded on religion, morals and patriotism" (Article 6), and that "the law shall preserve its legitimate entity and strengthen its ties and values". Feminist organisations perceive this amendment as a step to strengthen the traditional view of women as mothers and individuals in need of protection.

Such difficulties notwithstanding, the governments of the countries under review have taken several steps to modernise the legislative framework in support of women's rights. Moreover, some new laws are under preparation or have been adopted to take account of the constitutional changes. For instance, following the constitutional provision on violence, Egypt adopted a law in 2014 to combat violence against women in the form of sexual harassment in public places, and Tunisia is drafting a similar law.

Another example relates to women's political participation. The Tunisian law on elections of 2014 established the rule of alternating male and female candidates on electoral lists following the constitution's provision that the state shall guarantee the representation of women in elected bodies.[16] In June 2016, Tunisia adopted a gender parity bill for local elections that guarantees an equal number of male and female list leaders.

Application of international conventions and constitutional provisions by domestic courts

The existence of rights can contribute to the real strengthening of women's status only if violations of their rights are punished. The courts play a critical role in allowing women to demand that their rights be respected by their family (family law), their employer (labour law) or by business partners, clients and rival companies (business law), and in ensuring that legal provisions are implemented.

Articles 2(b) and 2(c) of CEDAW contain an implied obligation to provide effective recourse for women whose human rights have been violated. In the words of the CEDAW Committee, "States Parties must ensure that women can invoke the principle of equality in support of complaints of acts of discrimination contrary to the Convention, committed by public officials or by private actors. States Parties must further ensure that women have recourse to affordable, accessible and timely remedies, with legal aid and assistance as necessary, to be settled in a fair hearing by a competent and independent court or tribunal, where appropriate." (CEDAW, 2010a).

International conventions before domestic courts

The six States Parties to the CEDAW and ILO conventions have made progress in incorporating internationally agreed standards into their constitutions, and to various degrees into national legislation. As noted above, however, some domestic laws are not in line with various standards of these conventions. In such cases, national judges may have to decide which text to apply when a plaintiff files a claim in a domestic court.

The legal value of international conventions in domestic law differs among countries. Algeria,[17] Morocco,[18] Tunisia[19] and Libya[20] award them a supra-legislative value, meaning that the international treaty prevails in the case of a contradiction with domestic legislation. The Jordanian constitution does not address the legal value of the ratified international conventions, but the judiciary has established the principle of supremacy of international conventions above domestic law (Tamkeen, 2015). In Egypt, treaty provisions are on an equal legal footing with national laws;[21] in the case of conflict between the treaty and a statute, the most recent norm will prevail.

Yet all six States Parties to CEDAW have acknowledged to the Committee that their courts have hardly applied that convention. Neither Egypt nor Libya[22] nor Algeria provided cases where the CEDAW provisions had been directly invoked in court. Other countries have issued relevant rulings. For example, Jordan cited one case where a court referred to the convention: a girl had been allowed to change her first name on the grounds that her father had chosen the name without consulting her mother, and the judge ruled that the father's actions constituted a form of gender-based discrimination (CEDAW, 2012c). In 2000, the Tunis Court of First Instance rejected a request to enforce an Egyptian act of repudiation on the grounds that "repudiation constitutes a traditional and religious form of dissolving a marriage based on the unilateral will of the husband, with no consideration of the interests of the family, and consequently contradicts the Tunisian legal order, the 1948 Universal Declaration of Human Rights, as well as CEDAW" (CEDAW, 2010c).

The CEDAW Committee regularly urges state parties to take all appropriate measures to ensure that the convention is sufficiently known and applied by all branches of government, including the judiciary. It should be considered as a framework for all laws, court decisions and policies on gender equality and the empowerment of women. The committee also urges States Parties to enhance women's awareness of their rights, including through legal-literacy programmes and legal assistance, and to provide them with information on the convention in all parts of the country.[23]

Constitutional provisions before domestic courts

The constitutions of Algeria, Egypt, Jordan, Morocco and Tunisia provide for the establishment or reorganisation of constitutional courts to review the conformity of domestic laws with the constitution. Each has its own method for raising questions of constitutionality before its constitutional court. None allows its constitutional court to raise a constitutional issue at its own initiative, nor may individuals bring a case to the court directly. In Algeria (Article 182), Jordan (Article 60), Morocco (Article 132) and Tunisia (Article 120), judicial review can take place before a law is promulgated at the request of certain political bodies. If the court declares the law unconstitutional, the text cannot be promulgated. In Libya, the Supreme Court serves both as a constitutional court and a court of cassation.

Individuals in Algeria,[24] Egypt,[25] Jordan,[26] Morocco[27] and Tunisia[28] may challenge laws after their entry into force via a civil, penal, or administrative case in an ordinary court. In all these countries, a case can be brought to the constitutional court by the ordinary court itself or by litigants with the approval of these courts. This means that if the ordinary court believes that a law is valid, it can decline to refer it to the constitutional judge. If the court questions the constitutionality of the law, however, it can suspend examination of the litigation and refer the question to the constitutional court.

The ordinary court will suspend the litigation until the constitutional court resolves the constitutional question. The examination then resumes, according to the decision of the constitutional court. If the law is ruled constitutional, the ordinary judge will apply it to the pending case. If the constitutional court declares the law unconstitutional, however, it will cease to have legal effect and the ordinary judge will not be allowed to apply it to the pending case or any future case. The legislature will have to adopt a new law to fill the legal gap.

During examination of a personal status case before an ordinary court handling personal status matters (civil or family court, depending on the country), a woman is able, with the assent of the ordinary judge, to challenge the constitutionality of a family law provision that allegedly discriminates against her, as the constitutions of the six states bar discrimination on the basis of gender. The same is true for courts dealing with labour conflicts, where a woman employee in conflict with her employer can allege unconstitutionality of a labour law provision that discriminates among workers on the basis of gender.

Constitutional judges in the six countries will take into account different constitutional provisions, including those inspired by religious, cultural or societal values such as "Islam is the religion of the State"[29] or "the principles of the Islamic Sharia are the main source of legislation".[30] In practice, the legal effects of the new constitutional gender-related provisions therefore depend on the interpretation that the constitutional judges give to these sometimes conflicting provisions. As of July 2016, constitutional courts had not yet been created in Morocco and Tunisia. In the other countries, the constitutional courts had not issued any ruling on gender-discriminating laws under the new constitutions.

Gender balance in the appointment of constitutional judges would be highly desirable. The number of women constitutional judges remains extremely limited, however. In Egypt, the only woman member of the Supreme Constitutional Court was dismissed in 2012 when

Table 2.3. **Judicial review and constitutional courts**

	Who has access to the court?	Who are the members of the court?
Algeria	• *before promulgation of the law*: political bodies (president of the republic, president of the Council of the Nation, president of the National Assembly, prime minister or 50 deputies, or 30 members of the Council of the Nation)[1] • *after promulgation of the law*: the Supreme Court or State Council on the request of a litigant[2]	12 members: 4 appointed by the president of the republic, including its president; 2 elected by the People's National Assembly; 2 elected by the Council of the Nation; 2 elected by the Supreme Court; and 2 elected by the State Council[3]
Egypt	• *after promulgation of the law*: litigants, with the approval of the ordinary court[4] or directly by the ordinary courts[5]	"Sufficient number" of judges[6]: co-optation + officially nominated by president of the republic[7]
Jordan	• *before promulgation of the law*: political bodies (parliament or cabinet)[8] • *after promulgation of the law*: ordinary courts, on the request of litigants[9]	At least 9 judges (including the president)[10]: appointed by the king[11]
Morocco	• *before promulgation of the law*: political bodies (the king, the head of government, the president of the Chamber of Representatives, the president of the Chamber of Councillors, or 1/5 of the members of the Chamber of Representatives or 1/4 of the members of the Chamber of Councillors)[12] • *after promulgation of the law*: litigants[13]	12 judges[14]: 6 members designated by the king and 6 members elected, half by the Chamber of Representatives, and half by the Chamber of Councillors[15]
Tunisia	• *before promulgation of the law*: political bodies (president of the republic, head of government, president of the parliament or 30 members of parliament)[16] • *after promulgation of the law*: ordinary courts on the request of litigants[17]	12 judges: 4 appointed by the president of the republic, 4 by the Assembly of the Representatives of the People, and 4 by the Supreme Judicial Council[18]

Notes:

1. Article 187 of the 2016 Algerian Constitution. Algeria has a Constitutional Council, not a court, but it performs the same functions as a proper court.
2. Article 188 of the 2016 Algerian Constitution.
3. Article 183 of the 2016 Algerian Constitution.
4. Article 29 of Egypt's 1979 Law on the Supreme Constitutional Court.
5. Article 29 of Egypt's 1979 Law on the Supreme Constitutional Court.
6. Article 193 of the 2014 Egyptian Constitution and Article 3 of the 1979 Law on the Supreme Constitutional Court.
7. Articles 4 and 5 of Egypt's 1979 Law on the Supreme Constitutional Court.
8. Article 60 of the 1952 Jordanian Constitution, as amended in 2011.
9. Article 60 of the 1952 Jordanian Constitution, as amended in 2011.
10. Article 58 of the 1952 Jordanian Constitution, as amended in 2011.
11. Article 58 of the 1952 Jordanian Constitution, as amended in 2011.
12. Article 130 of the 2011 Moroccan Constitution.
13. Article 130 of the 2011 Moroccan Constitution.
14. Article 132 of the 2011 Moroccan Constitution.
15. Article 133 of the 2011 Moroccan Constitution.
16. Article 120 of the 2014 Tunisian Constitution.
17. Article 120 of the 2014 Tunisian Constitution.
18. Article 118 of the 2014 Tunisian Constitution.

the new constitution limited the number of its judges to 11. No woman was reappointed when that constitution was abolished in July 2013. In Algeria, two of the nine current members are women. There is no woman on the Jordanian Constitutional Court (Table 2.3).

Citizens' right to file claims in court

Civil courts are competent to decide upon labour conflicts. Civil servants bring their conflicts before administrative courts, where these exist (Algeria, Egypt). Most business law conflicts are brought before the commercial sections of civil courts. Civil courts also adjudicate in other conflicts. In Morocco, for example, the code of criminal procedure was revised in 2002 to repeal a provision (Article 336) that granted husbands spousal immunity absent judicial consent to the contrary.

Courts have been secularised in the six countries. In Jordan, however, family law issues continue to be submitted to religious courts. The absence of women in these courts and the religious education of the judges are likely to produce a conservative view of family relations.

A greater number of women throughout the court system is essential to ensuring the application and safeguarding of rights without gender bias; gender diversity helps courts understand the real-world implications of their rulings. In Jordan, only 16% of judges are women; the figure rises to 24% in Morocco, more than 36% in Tunisia, 39% in Libya and almost 40% in Algeria (according to the respective country reports). In Egypt, there are still very few women on the bench in civil courts and none on the state council, which is in charge of administrative litigation (between individuals and administrative bodies). Women remain the minority in the most senior positions of the judicial system in all six countries.

Various barriers may obstruct the use of existing legal and judicial mechanisms to enforce women's rights and gender equality in labour, business and family affairs. Focus group participants[31] underscored that social pressures and customs dissuade many women from claiming their rights in court, as they fear scandal, social exclusion and stigma. In addition, as a case may be filed against members of the family upon whom women rely financially, they do their utmost to settle disputes out of court (Figure 2.1). Some change was acknowledged during discussions in Morocco, however, particularly in litigation regarding the respect of economic rights in divorce cases, which women were taking to court.

Figure 2.1. **Reasons for not filing a case in court, by gender (Jordan)**

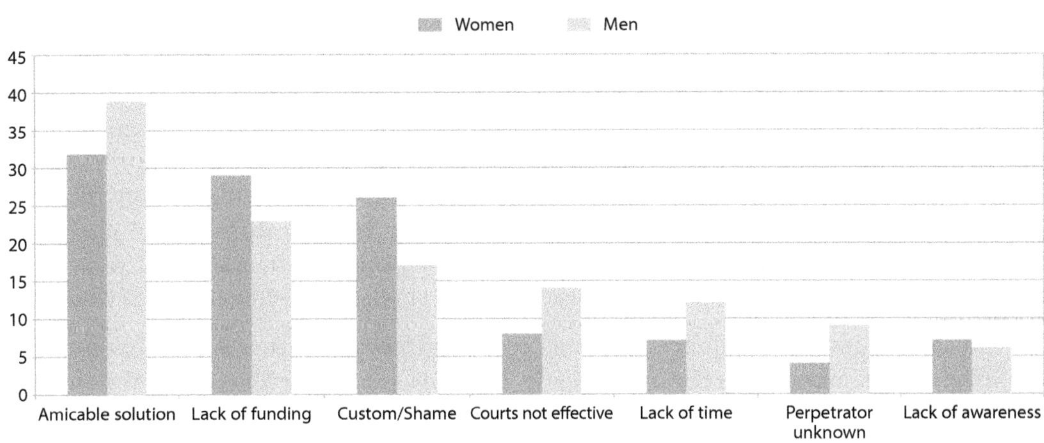

Source: World Bank (2013), "Country gender assessment: Economic participation, agency and access to justice in Jordan".

Women also hesitate to resort to court due to long and burdensome processes including filing claims, navigating the procedure and implementing the court decision. They are also concerned by gender bias within the justice system and fear that the lengthy procedures may not achieve the expected results (Box 2.5). Establishing courts competent for minor litigation, where procedures are simplified and costs reduced when less than a specified monetary threshold is at issue, can encourage women to access courts, and business women in particular.[32] In Morocco, Libya, Jordan, Tunisia and Egypt, there are either small-claims courts, which hear only civil cases between private litigants, or fast-track procedures for cases of more general jurisdiction. The simplified procedures can be exploited only when the monetary value of the dispute is below a certain percentage of gross national income (GNI) per capita, which hence constitutes a threshold.[33]

Box 2.5. **Stereotyping and gender bias in the justice system**

Stereotyping and gender bias in the justice system have far-reaching consequences on women's full enjoyment of their rights. They impede women's access to justice in all areas of the law, and may particularly affect female victims of violence. Stereotyping distorts perceptions and results in decisions based on preconceived beliefs and myths rather than relevant facts. Often judges adopt rigid standards about what they consider to be appropriate behaviour for women and penalise those who do not conform. Stereotyping also affects the credibility given to women's testimony as parties or witnesses. Such stereotyping can cause judges to misinterpret or misapply laws. This has far-reaching consequences, for example, in criminal law, where it results in perpetrators' not being held legally accountable for violations of women's rights, thereby upholding a culture of impunity. In all areas of the law, stereotyping compromises the impartiality and integrity of the justice system, which can, in turn, lead to miscarriages of justice, including the revictimisation of plaintiffs.

Judges, magistrates and adjudicators are not the only actors in the justice system who apply, reinforce and perpetuate stereotypes. Prosecutors, law enforcement officials and other actors often allow stereotypes to influence investigations and trials, especially in cases of gender-based violence, with stereotypes undermining the claims of the victim/survivor and simultaneously supporting the defences advanced by the alleged perpetrator. Stereotyping, therefore, permeates both the investigation and trial phases and finally shapes the judgement.

Women should be able to rely on a justice system free of myths and stereotypes, and on a judiciary whose impartiality is not compromised by biased assumptions. Eliminating judicial stereotyping in the justice system is a crucial step in ensuring equality and justice for victims and survivors.

Source: CEDAW (2010a), *General Recommendation on Women's Access to Justice.*

In family law cases in Jordan,[34] Libya[35] and Egypt,[36] two female witnesses are required as the equivalent to one male witness. Women therefore face the difficulty of providing evidence when a witness statement from two men (or from one man and two women) is required. This is the case when women need to prove spousal abuse in a divorce claim.

Judicial processes run up costs such as court and lawyers' fees. A lack of financial resources forms another barrier, particularly for poor women or those in low-paid and precarious jobs. To overcome this, people on a low income, particularly women, are eligible for legal aid in Morocco, Egypt and Libya. The focus groups highlighted, however, that in many cases women are unaware of potential support for access to justice. They also may not know about their rights and entitlements or the redress available in case of violation of their rights. Legal-empowerment strategies and rights-awareness programmes would improve access to justice for women and increase their capacity to exercise their rights.

In Egypt, the Ministry of Justice and the UN Development Programme (UNDP) have agreed to introduce legal aid offices and to enhance the skills and knowledge of staffers of the dispute-settlement office. The project aims to raise awareness among citizens about contacting courts, and to improve the institutional and human capacity of the judicial sector by introducing the legal-aid concept and strengthening the mediation function of family courts.[37] The offices provide immediate pro bono access to justice and legal advice and information about rights within family law. They target disadvantaged people, including women, who fear going to court and are inclined to avoid exercising their right of access to justice because of the time involved and the cost (Khafagy & Shami, 2014).

As a consequence of impediments to access to justice, citizens may prefer to claim their rights through informal justice systems. These systems may be more accessible than formal mechanisms and may have the potential to provide quick, relatively inexpensive and culturally relevant remedies. They may deal with issues that have a direct bearing on the interests of women (and children), such as issues of customary marriage, custody, dissolution of marriage, inheritance and property rights.[38]

Box 2.6. **Effective government tools for gender mainstreaming**

The adoption of laws that explicitly provide for gender equality in economic activities, while essential, is not sufficient to ensure women's economic empowerment. Key elements of gender-responsive policy and governance infrastructure must be mainstreamed into public policies in order to address the persistent gender-equality gap. Key components of gender mainstreaming, which some of the governments have introduced, include:

- A vision and strategy for gender equality

In the MENA region over the past decade, many countries have developed a mainstreaming strategy, either as a document beyond the broader gender-equality strategy, for example Tunisia's "*Stratégie de la lutte contre la violence à l'égard des femmes au sein de la famille et de la société*", or embedded in a broader strategy, for instance Morocco's "Agenda gouvernemental pour l'égalité 2011-2015".

- Institutional capacities and gender institutions

Governments need a sound public-sector capacity and institutional framework. This includes the design of gender institutions, with clear delineation of their responsibilities, and mechanisms for accountability and compliance with gender-equality requirements. Institutions for promoting gender equality and mainstreaming are located at highest political level, either in a single ministry with a combined portfolio, as in Tunisia, Morocco and Algeria, or within a single ministry or institution (council, commission) under the aegis of the prime minister or president, as in Jordan and Egypt. Moreover, to embed gender considerations and strengthen the capacity for developing effective gender-related initiatives, most MENA countries have established gender-equality units and staff in line ministries across the government. For example, Jordan's National Committee for Women has established gender focal points in several public institutions, including the ministries of planning, finance, and education, as well as the department of statistics and other agencies. Ombudsman offices, as in Egypt, ensure that gender-equality initiatives have their intended impact.

Box 2.6. **Effective government tools for gender mainstreaming** *(continued)*

- Gender impact assessment and public consultation

Policies run the risk of inadvertently discriminating against women by not taking into account their different impacts on men and women. MENA countries increasingly undertake gender analysis of their strategies, policies and laws. Morocco and Jordan, for example, report on the use of gender analysis to legislatures or legislative committees, and Jordan integrates gender analysis into the regulatory impact assessment. Moreover, it is important for all MENA governments to consult women themselves about their priorities and concerns in order systematically to resolve the most pressing issues across the region and to ensure that national priorities on gender equality reflect the views and needs of various groups across the population.

- Gender-responsive budgeting (GRB) as a specific method for gender impact assessment

The development of data related to gender budgeting and the capacity to analyse budgets from a gender perspective, while initially resource intensive, has the advantage of quickly identifying gaps in gender equality and areas for improvement, in line with broader gender-equality and gender mainstreaming strategies. Morocco provides a leading example of gender budgeting in the MENA region. The government gradually introduced a gender dimension into ministerial department budgets, and gender-budgeting capacity has been progressively decentralised. Since 2007, several ministerial departments have created their own programmes to incorporate gender into budgeting at the local level.

Source: OECD (2014), Women in Public: Life Gender, Law and Policy in the Middle East and North Africa, OECD, Paris.

Conclusions

The six countries under review are parties to a number of international conventions that establish principles of human rights as well as specific standards on gender equality. These international conventions provide a vision for attaining women's empowerment through their ability to exercise their rights, make decisions for themselves and generate income. Taking account of these international benchmarks on women's economic empowerment, the constitutions of the six countries now integrate core concepts of gender equality and non-discrimination; the right to participate in public and private life; and the protection of women's physical integrity.

These countries have introduced new laws supporting gender equality into the different codes that affect women's economic empowerment, namely family, labour and business law. In order for these laws to be effective and ensure gender equality, they must be known and implemented so that appropriate measures may be taken in cases of failure to apply the law.

Although women can file claims in court, provided they are aware of their rights, access to justice remains problematic. Barriers include legal formalities that are not always favourable to women and the cost of going to court as well as social pressure, with many women dissuaded from claiming their rights for fear of scandal, social exclusion and stigma. For this reason, action is needed both on the demand side – raising women's awareness of their legal rights and demanding proper enforcement of the law – and on the supply side – strengthening the response capacity of the legal system.

Recommendations

Governments are encouraged to:

- Lift their reservations to CEDAW and ratify the additional protocol, if they have not already done so, and incorporate a definition of gender-based discrimination, and an explicit prohibition of such discrimination, into the constitution and other relevant domestic legislation, in line with CEDAW's Article 1, when this has not yet been done.
- Ensure that international conventions and related commitments are incorporated into the constitution and embedded in the national legal system.
- Ensure the application of constitutional provisions that encourage women's involvement in political and economic activities and ensure diversity in those activities, including in the judiciary through a stronger participation of women judges; develop policies that promote equality in these domains; and monitor implementation of the principle of gender equality.
- Reinforce knowledge among judges, magistrates, lawyers and other legal professionals about international conventions that the government has ratified by making the conventions an integral part of legal education and training.
- Take measures to eliminate gender stereotyping, including awareness raising and capacity building for all actors of the justice system, and incorporate a legal culture supportive of gender equality and non-discrimination in all aspects of the justice system.
- Create a legal, social and political environment that promotes and supports access to justice by women, including through broad legal empowerment and legal-aid services at an affordable price; where not yet in place establish courts competent for minor litigation of relatively low value (small-claims courts) with simplified procedures; reinforce control and monitoring mechanisms to ensure legislation is implemented.
- Consider signing up to the 2013 OECD Council Recommendation on Gender Equality in Education, Employment and Entrepreneurship and the 2015 OECD Council Recommendation on Gender Equality in Public Life.

Notes

1. Article 2 of the UDHR declares the general entitlement to the rights and freedoms it sets forth without distinction of any kind, including sex. This entitlement applies to Article 23(1), which declares the right to free choice of employment and protection against unemployment, as well as Article 24, which declares the right to reasonable limitation of working hours and periodic holidays with pay.
2. Tunisia has adopted a general declaration, which has a similar power, as a general reservation: "The Tunisian government declares that it shall not adopt any administrative or legislative decision by virtue of the convention if it is likely to go against the first chapter of the Tunisian Constitution." Chapter 1 contains Article 1, which states that "Tunisia is a free state…its religion is Islam."

3. The CEDAW Committee "considers Article 2 to represent the very essence of the obligations of participating States as required by the Convention. As a result, the committee considers the reservations to Article 2 or its sub-paragraphs to be in conflict with the purpose and the objective of the Convention and, therefore, do not authorise these reservations, in accordance with Paragraph 2 of Article 28. State parties that have entered reservations to Article 2 or to sub-paragraphs of Article 2 should explain the practical effect of those reservations on the implementation of the Convention and should indicate the steps taken to keep the reservations under review, with the goal of withdrawing them as soon as possible." (CEDAW Committee, General Recommendation no. 28, par. 41, 16 December 2010.

4. Statement on Reservations to the Convention on the Elimination of all Forms of Discrimination against Women on Reservations to CEDAW adopted by the Committee on the Elimination of Discrimination against Women, 1998, www.ohchr.org/Documents/HRBodies/CEDAW/Statements/StatementsOnReservationsEnglish.pdf; Status of the Convention on the Elimination of all Forms of Discrimination Against Women, https://treaties.un.org/Pages/ViewDetails.aspx?src=TREATY&mtdsg_no=IV-8&chapter=4&lang=en#EndDec.

5. ILO, ILO Supervisory system/mechanism, www.ilo.org/global/standards/applying-and-promoting-international-labour-standards/committee-of-experts-on-the-application-of-conventions-and-recommendations/lang--en/index.htm.

6. ILO, CEACR, Discrimination (Employment and Occupation) Convention, Observation on Algeria, 2014, www.ilo.org/dyn/normlex/en/f?p=1000:13100:0::NO:13100:P13100_COMMENT_ID,P11110_COUNTRY_ID,P11110_COUNTRY_NAME,P11110_COMMENT_YEAR:3177174,102908,Algeria,2014.

7. ILO, CEACR, Discrimination (Employment and Occupation) Convention, Observation on Morocco, 2014, www.ilo.org/dyn/normlex/en/f?p=1000:13100:0::NO:13100:P13100_COMMENT_ID,P11110_COUNTRY_ID,P11110_COUNTRY_NAME,P11110_COMMENT_YEAR:3145222,102993,Morocco,2013.

8. ILO, Equal Remuneration Convention, Observation on Egypt, www.ilo.org/dyn/normlex/en/f?p=1000:13100:0::NO:13100:P13100_COMMENT_ID,P11110_COUNTRY_ID,P11110_COUNTRY_NAME,P11110_COMMENT_YEAR:3058256,102915,Egypt,2012.

9. ILO, CEACR, Discrimination (Employment and Occupation) Convention, Observation to Jordan, 2013, www.ilo.org/dyn/normlex/en/f?p=1000:13100:0::NO:13100:P13100_COMMENT_ID,P11110_COUNTRY_ID,P11110_COUNTRY_NAME,P11110_COMMENT_YEAR:3145506,103201,Jordan,2013.

10. ILO, CEACR, Discrimination (Employment and Occupation) Convention, Observation to Libya, www.ilo.org/dyn/normlex/en/f?p=1000:13100:0::NO:13100:P13100_COMMENT_ID,P11110_COUNTRY_ID,P11110_COUNTRY_NAME,P11110_COMMENT_YEAR:2310225,103130,Libya,2009.

11. ILO, CEACR, Discrimination (Employment and Occupation) Convention, Observation on Tunisia, 2014, www.ilo.org/dyn/normlex/en/f?p=1000:13100:0::NO:13100:P13100_COMMENT_ID,P11110_COUNTRY_ID,P11110_COUNTRY_NAME,P11110_COMMENT_YEAR:3186812,102986,Tunisia,2014.

12. A draft permanent constitution was presented in April 2016 by the Constituent Assembly elected in 2013, but it had not been put to referendum by July 2016 due to the precarious current circumstances and civil war in the country.

13. Female participation in the 2012 Egyptian Constituent Assembly was 6%, against 10% in the drafting committee of the 2014 Egyptian constitution. No woman was appointed in Jordan to the Royal Commission in spite of intense lobbying by civil society. In Libya, a quota of 10% was allocated to women in the Constituent Assembly. In Tunisia, in contrast, women made up 49 of the 217 members elected to the Constituent Assembly, meaning they held 24% of the seats.

14. However, the same article adds that "this is in accordance with the provisions of the constitution, the constants of the Kingdom and of its laws." It is up to judges to interpret "the constants of the Kingdom".
15. In March 2015, the government approved the creation of the agency, and a law to establish it was approved by the parliament in May 2016. The authority is not operational yet.
16. Article 24 of the Law of 2014 regarding elections and referenda.
17. Article 150 of the 2016 Algerian Constitution.
18. Preamble of the 2011 Moroccan Constitution.
19. Article 20 of the 2014 Tunisian Constitution.
20. Article 23 of the Libyan Civil Code issued in 1954.
21. Article 93 of the 2014 Egyptian Constitution.
22. Libya declared to the CEDAW Committee that "because Libyan legislation, which is also binding for domestic courts, is consistent with the principles of the Convention, there have not been cases in which the provisions of the Convention have been invoked" (CEDAW, 2009).
23. See for instance CEDAW, 2010d, p. 4.
24. Article 188 of the 2016 Algerian Constitution.
25. Article 29b of the 1979 Law on the Supreme Constitutional Court. In Morocco, the court had not yet been established as to July 2016.
26. Article 60 of the 1952 Jordanian Constitution, as amended in 2011.
27. Article 133 of the 2011 Moroccan Constitution.
28. Article 120 and 123 of the Tunisian Constitution.
29. Article 2 of the 2016 Algerian Constitution, Article 3 of the 2011 Moroccan Constitution, Article 2 of the 1952 Jordanian Constitution, Article 1 of the 2011 Libyan Constitutional Declaration, Article 2 of the 2014 Egyptian Constitution. In Tunisia, Article 1 of the 2014 Constitution states: "Tunisia is a free, independent, sovereign state; its religion is Islam, its language is Arabic, and its system is republican."
30. Article 2 of the 2014 Egyptian Constitution.
31. For more information concerning the methodology and participant demography in the focus groups, see Annex A.
32. This is the case in Egypt, where "summary" or "partial" courts rule in criminal matters on petty offenses and misdemeanours and in civil matters on cases involving amounts less than EGP 10 000 (Egyptian pounds).
33. The percentage in Morocco equals 4%, 12% in Libya, 26% in Jordan, 92% in Tunisia, and 171% in Egypt (Women, Business and the Law 2016 database).
34. Article 127 of the Jordanian 2010 Personal Status Law.
35. Article 72 of the 1984 Libyan Personal Status Law.
36. This is not directly stated in the personal status laws, but is derived by judges from the fact that in case something is not regulated directly, Islamic law applies in this area of law.
37. During the period 2009-12, the total number of litigants who sought the services of the legal aid offices was estimated at 22 747, of whom more than 61% were women.
38. UN WOMEN, UNDP, UNICEF: Informal Justice Systems charting a course for human rights-based engagement www.unicef.org/protection/INFORMAL_JUSTICE_SYSTEMS.pdf.

References

Bahdi, R. (2007), "Background paper on women's access to justice in the MENA region", for International Development Research Centre, Women's Rights and Citizenship Program and the Middle East Regional Office, Middle East and North African Regional Consultation, Cairo, www.uwindsor.ca/law/rbahdi/sites/uwindsor.ca.law.rbahdi/files/womens_access_to_justice_in_mena-bahdi_en.pdf.

Brotman, S. et al. (2008), *Implementing CEDAW in North Africa and the Middle East: Roadblocks and Victories*, Middle East and North Africa (Mena) Report, http://pages.uoregon.edu/aweiss/intl421_521/CEDAW_Report_MENAf.pdf.

Byrnes, A. (2012), "Article 2", in *The UN Convention on the Elimination of All Forms of Discrimination Against Women: A Commentary*, Marsha A. Freeman, Christine Chinkin and Beate Rudolf (eds.), Oxford Commentaries on International Law, Oxford.

CEDAW (2012a), "Responses of Algeria to the list of issues to be taken up in connection with the consideration of its combined third and fourth periodic report", UN Committee on the Elimination of Discrimination Against Women (CEDAW), http://tbinternet.ohchr.org/_layouts/treatybodyexternal/Download.aspx?symbolno=CEDAW%2fC%2fDZA%2fQ%2f3-4%2fAdd.1&Lang=en.

CEDAW (2012b), "Concluding observations of the Committee on the Elimination of Discrimination against Women (Algeria)", UN Committee on the Elimination of Discrimination Against Women (CEDAW), http://tbinternet.ohchr.org/_layouts/treatybodyexternal/Download.aspx?symbolno=CEDAW%2fC%2fDZA%2fCO%2f3-4&Lang=en.

CEDAW (2012c), "Responses of Jordan to the list of issues to be taken up in connection with the consideration of its fifth periodic report", UN Committee on the Elimination of Discrimination Against Women (CEDAW), http://tbinternet.ohchr.org/_layouts/treatybodyexternal/Download.aspx?symbolno=CEDAW%2fC%2fJOR%2fQ%2f5%2fAdd.1&Lang=en.

CEDAW (2012d), "Concluding observations (Jordan)", UN Committee on the Elimination of Discrimination Against Women (CEDAW), http://tbinternet.ohchr.org/_layouts/treatybodyexternal/Download.aspx?symbolno=CEDAW%2fC%2fJOR%2fCO%2f5&Lang=en.

CEDAW (2010a), "General recommendation No. 28 on the core obligations of States Parties under Article 2 of the Convention on the Elimination of All Forms of Discrimination against Women," UN Committee on the Elimination of Discrimination Against Women (CEDAW), http://www2.ohchr.org/english/bodies/cedaw/docs/CEDAW-C-2010-47-GC2.pdf.

CEDAW (2010b), "Combined third and fourth periodic reports of States Parties (Algeria), 24 March 2010," UN Committee on the Elimination of Discrimination Against Women (CEDAW), http://tbinternet.ohchr.org/_layouts/treatybodyexternal/Download.aspx?symbolno=CEDAW%2fC%2fDZA%2f3-4&Lang=en.

CEDAW (2010c), "Written replies from the government of Tunisia to the list of issues and questions with regard to the consideration of the combined fifth and sixth periodic reports," UN Committee on the Elimination of Discrimination Against Women (CEDAW), http://tbinternet.ohchr.org/_layouts/treatybodyexternal/Download.aspx?symbolno=CEDAW%2fC%2fTUN%2fQ%2f6%2fAdd.1&Lang=en.

CEDAW (2010d), "Concluding observations (Egypt)", UN Committee on the Elimination of Discrimination Against Women (CEDAW), http://tbinternet.ohchr.org/_layouts/treatybodyexternal/Download.aspx?symbolno=CEDAW%2fC%2fEGY%2fCO%2f7&Lang=en.

CEDAW (2010e), "Concluding observations (Tunisia)", UN Committee on the Elimination of Discrimination Against Women (CEDAW), p. 2, http://tbinternet.ohchr.org/_layouts/treatybodyexternal/Download.aspx?symbolno=CEDAW%2fC%2fTUN%2fCO%2f6&Lang=en.

CEDAW (2009), "Responses to the list of issues and questions with regard to the consideration of the second periodic report (Libya)", UN Committee on the Elimination of Discrimination Against Women (CEDAW) http://tbinternet.ohchr.org/_layouts/treatybodyexternal/Download.aspx?symbolno=CEDAW%2fC%2fLBY%2fQ%2f2%2fAdd.1&Lang=en.

CEDAW (2008), "Combined sixth and seventh periodic reports of States Parties (Egypt)," UN Committee on the Elimination of Discrimination Against Women (CEDAW), http://tbinternet.ohchr.org/_layouts/treatybodyexternal/Download.aspx?symbolno=CEDAW%2fC%2fEGY%2f7&Lang=en.

CEDAW (2007a), "Responses to the list of issues and questions with regard to the consideration of the combined third and fourth periodic reports (Morocco)," UN Committee on the Elimination of Discrimination Against Women (CEDAW), http://tbinternet.ohchr.org/_layouts/treatybodyexternal/Download.aspx?symbolno=CEDAW%2fC%2fMAR%2fQ%2f4%2fAdd.1&Lang=en.

CEDAW (2007b), "Responses to the list of issues and questions with regard to the consideration of the combined third and fourth periodic reports (Morocco)," UN Committee on the Elimination of Discrimination Against Women (CEDAW), http://tbinternet.ohchr.org/_layouts/treatybodyexternal/Download.aspx?symbolno=CEDAW%2fC%2fMAR%2fQ%2f4%2fAdd.1&Lang=en.

CEDAW (2006), "Combined third and fourth reports of States Parties (Jordan)," 10 March 2006, UN Committee on the Elimination of Discrimination Against Women (CEDAW), http://tbinternet.ohchr.org/_layouts/treatybodyexternal/Download.aspx?symbolno=CEDAW%2fC%2fJOR%2f3-4&Lang=en.

CEDAW (2003), "Second periodic report of Algeria to the CEDAW," UN Committee on the Elimination of Discrimination Against Women (CEDAW), https://documents-dds-ny.un.org/doc/UNDOC/GEN/N03/247/53/PDF/N0324753.pdf?OpenElement.

CEDAW (1998), "Statement on reservations to the Convention on the Elimination of all Forms of Discrimination against Women adopted by the Committee on the Elimination of Discrimination Against Women", www.ohchr.org/Documents/HRBodies/CEDAW/Statements/StatementsOnReservationsEnglish.pdf.

Council of Europe (2015), *Compilation of Good Practices to Reduce Existing Obstacles and Facilitate Women's Access to Justice*, Gender Equality Commission, Council of Europe, https://rm.coe.int/CoERMPublicCommonSearchServices/DisplayDCTMContent?documentId=0900001680597b12.

Cusack S. (2014), *Eliminating Judicial Stereotyping: Equal Access to Justice for Women in Gender-Based Violence Cases*, Commissioned by the UN Office of the High Commissioner for Human Rights.

Cusack S. and L. Pusey (2013), "CEDAW and the rights to non-discrimination and equality", *Melbourne Journal of International Law*, Vol. 14/1, Melbourne, Australia.

Cusack S. and R.J. Cook (2012), "Combating Discrimination against Women", in Krause, C. and M. Scheinin (eds.), *International Protection of Human Rights: A Textbook*, 2nd ed., Institute for Human Rights, Åbo Akademic University, Åbo, Finland, pp. 211-242.

Cusack S. and R.J. Cook (2009), "Combating Discrimination Based on Sex and Gender", in Krause, C. and M. Scheinin (eds.), *International Protection of Human Rights: A Textbook*, Institute for Human Rights, Åbo Akademic University, Åbo, Finland, pp. 205-226.

Douglas, S. (2007), "Gender equality and justice programming: Equitable access to justice for women", *UNDP Primers in Gender and Democratic Governance*, No. 2, UNDP, New York, www.undp.org/content/undp/en/home/librarypage/womens-empowerment/gender-equality-and-justice-programming-equitable-access-to-justice-for-women1.html.

ESCWA (2014), "Access to justice for women and girls in the Arab region: From ratification to implementation of international instruments", *Status of Arab Women Report,* United Nations Economic and Social Commission for Western Asia, Beirut, https://www.unescwa.org/sites/www.unescwa.org/files/publications/files/e_escwa_ecw_15_1_e.pdf.

Freeman, M.A. (2009), "Reservations to CEDAW: An analysis for UNICEF", *Discussion Paper*, United Nations Children's Fund (UNICEF), New York, www.unicef.org/gender/files/Reservations_to_CEDAW-an_Analysis_for_UNICEF.pdf.

International Development Law Organization (2013), "Accessing justice: Models, strategies and best practices on women's empowerment", International Development Law Organization, https://www.idlo.int/sites/default/files/Womens_Access_to_Justice_Full_Report.pdf.

Irving, H. (2008), *Gender and the Constitution: Equity and Agency in Comparative Constitutional Design*, Cambridge University Press, New York.

Khafagy F. and T. El Shami (2014), "Evaluation report of access to justice project", United Nations Development Programme, New York, www.eg.undp.org/content/dam/egypt/docs/Governance/LLAD%20Evaluation%202014.pdf.

OECD (2016), *2015 OECD Recommendation of the Council on Gender Equality in Public Life*, OECD Publishing, Paris, http://dx.doi.org/10.1787/9789264252820-en.

OECD (2014), *Women in Public Life: Gender, Law and Policy in the Middle East and North Africa*, OECD Publishing, Paris, http://dx.doi.org/10.1787/9789264224636-en.

OECD (2013), *Recommendation of the Council on Gender Equality in Education, Employment and Entrepreneurship*, www.oecd.org/gender/C-MIN(2013)5-ENG.pdf.

OECD (2012), *Closing the Gender Gap: Act Now*, OECD Publishing, Paris, http://dx.doi.org/10.1787/9789264179370-en.

Raday, F. (2012), "Women's access to justice", available from www.ohchr.org/Documents/HRBodies/CEDAW/AccesstoJustice/Ms.FrancesRaday.pdf.

Tamkeen (2015), *An Analytic Review of Jordanian Legislation Related to Anti-Trafficking*, www.tipheroes.org/media/1534/an-analytic-review-of-jordanian-legislation-related-to-anti-trafficking.pdf.

UN (2007), *Yearbook of the International Law Commission*, Vol. 1, United Nations Publications, New York and Geneva, http://legal.un.org/docs/?path=./ilc/publications/yearbooks/english/ilc_2007_v1.pdf&lang=EFSRA.

UN General Assembly (1966a), *International Covenant on Economic, Social and Cultural Rights*, United Nations, Treaty Series, Vol. 993, p. 3, www.refworld.org/docid/3ae6b36c0.html.

UN General Assembly (1966b), International Covenant on Civil and Political Rights, United Nations, Treaty Series, Vol. 999, p. 171, www.refworld.org/docid/3ae6b3aa0.html.

UN Women (2014), *Cairo Declaration*, League of Arab States, Cairo, Egypt, www.unwomen.org/~/media/headquarters/attachments/sections/csw/58/csw58-declaration-cairo-en%20pdf.ashx.

UN Women (2011), *Progress of the World's Women: In Pursuit of Justice*, www.unwomen.org/~/media/headquarters/attachments/sections/library/publications/2011/progressoftheworldswomen-2011-en.pdf.

UN WOMEN, UNDP, UNICEF (2013), *Informal Justice Systems: Charting a Course for Human Rights-Based Engagement*, www.unwomen.org/en/digital-library/publications/2013/1/informal-justice-systems-charting-a-course-for-human-rights-based-engagement.

World Bank (2016), "Women, Business and the Law 2016" (database), World Bank, Washington, DC, http://wbl.worldbank.org/~/media/WBG/WBL/Documents/Reports/2016/Women-Business-and-the-Law-2016.pdf.

World Bank (2013), "Country gender assessment: Economic participation, agency and access to justice in Jordan", World Bank, Washington, DC, http://documents.worldbank.org/curated/en/2013/07/18423362/country-gender-assessment-economic-participation-agency-access-justice-jordan.

Annex 2.A1

Main constitutional provisions on equality

The legal provisions set out below are based on unofficial translations.

Algeria

Article 32. All citizens are equal before the law without any discrimination due to birth, race, sex, opinion or any other personal or social condition or circumstance.

Article 34. The aim of institutions shall be to ensure equality of rights and duties for all citizens, both men and women, by removing the obstacles which hinder human progress and impede the effective participation of all in political, economic, social and cultural life.

Article 35. The State works for the promotion of the political rights of women by increasing their chances of access to representation in elected assemblies. The modes of enforcement of this article are to be laid down by organic law.

Article 36 (added in 2016). The State encourages parity between men and women on the labour market. The State encourages the promotion of women to responsibilities in institutions, public administrations as well as on the enterprise level.

Egypt

Article 9. The State shall ensure equal opportunities for all citizens without discrimination.

Article 11. The State shall ensure the achievement of equality between women and men in all civil, political, economic, social and cultural rights in accordance with the provisions of this constitution.

The State shall take the necessary measures to ensure the appropriate representation of women in the houses of representatives, as specified by law. The State shall also guarantee women's rights of holding public and senior management offices in the state, and their appointment in judicial bodies and authorities without discrimination.

The State shall protect women against all forms of violence and ensure enabling women to strike a balance between family duties and work requirements.

The State shall provide care to and protection of motherhood and childhood, female heads of families and elderly and neediest women.

Article 53. All citizens are equal before the law. They are equal in rights, freedoms and general duties, without discrimination based on religion, belief, sex, origin, race, colour, language, disability, social class, political or geographical affiliation or any other reason.

Discrimination and incitement of hatred is a crime punished by law.

The State shall take necessary measures for eliminating all forms of discrimination and the law shall regulate creating an independent commission for this purpose.

Jordan

Article 6.

1) Jordanians shall be equal before the law. There shall be no discrimination between them as regards to their rights and duties on grounds of race, language or religion.

[...]

3) The State shall ensure work and education within the limits of its possibilities, and shall ensure tranquillity and equal opportunities to all Jordanians.

4) The family is the basis of society, founded on religion, morals and patriotism; the law shall preserve its legitimate entity and strengthen its ties and values.

5) The law shall protect motherhood, childhood and the elderly and care for youth and the disabled and protect them from abuse and exploitation.

Libya

Article 6. Libyans shall be equal before the law. They shall enjoy equal civil and political rights, shall have the same opportunities in all areas and be subject to the same public duties and obligations, without distinction due to religion, belief, language, wealth, gender, kinship, political opinions, social status, or tribal, regional or familial loyalty.

Morocco

Article 19. Men and women have equal civil, political, economic, social, cultural and environmental rights and freedoms, as stated in this title and in other provisions of the constitution, as well as in the international conventions and covenants duly ratified by Morocco, with due regard to the provisions of the constitution and the constant and laws of the Kingdom.

The State endeavours to achieve gender parity. An Authority for Parity and the Struggle Against All Forms of Discrimination is established to this effect.

Tunisia

Article 21. All citizens, male and female, have equal rights and duties. They are equal before the law without any discrimination. The State guarantees individual and collective freedoms and rights to all citizens and provides the conditions for a dignified life.

Article 34. The rights of election, voting and candidacy are guaranteed, in accordance with the law. The State shall ensure the representation of women in elected assemblies.

Article 46. The State shall commit to protecting women's achieved rights and seek to support and develop them.

The State shall guarantee equal opportunities between women and men in the bearing of all the various responsibilities in all fields.

The State shall seek to achieve parity between women and men in elected councils.

The State shall also take all necessary measures to eliminate violence against women.

Annex 2.A2

Constitutional guarantees of the right to work

Algeria, Article 69 of the 2016 Constitution.

All citizens have the right to work.

The right to protection, safety and hygiene at work is guaranteed by law.

The right to rest is guaranteed; the law specifies the manner of its exercise.

The right of workers to social security is guaranteed by law.

The employment of children under 16 is punishable by law.

The State works to promote apprenticeship and implements policies in support of job creation.

Egypt, Article 12 of the 2014 Constitution.

Work is a right, duty and honour guaranteed by the State. No citizen may be forced to work except as required by Law and for the purpose of performing a public service for a fixed period in return for a fair consideration, and without prejudice to the basic rights of those obliged to carry out such work.

Jordan, Article 23 of the 1952 Constitution.

1) Work is the right of all citizens, and the State shall avail it to Jordanians by directing and improving the national economy.

2) The State shall protect labour and enact legislation therefore based on the following principles:

a) Giving the worker a wage commensurate with the quantity and quality of his work.

b) Defining weekly work hours and granting workers weekly and annual paid rest days.

c) Specifying special compensation to workers supporting families and in the cases of dismissal, illness, disability and emergencies arising out of work.

d) Establishing special conditions for the work of women and juveniles.

e) Subjection of factories to health safeguards.

f) Free trade unions within the limits of the law

Libya, Article 8 of the 2011 Constitutional Declaration.

The State shall ensure equal opportunity and strive to guarantee a proper standard of living, the right to work, education medical care and social security to every citizen. The State shall guarantee individual and private property. It shall guarantee the just distribution of national wealth among citizens and among the different cities and regions of the State.

Morocco, Article 31 of the 2011 Constitution.

The State, public establishments and territorial collectivities work for the mobilisation of all means available to facilitate the equal access of citizens [feminine] and citizens [masculine] to conditions that permit their enjoyment of the right:

- to health care;
- to social protection, medical coverage and mutualist or state-sponsored solidarity;
- to modern, accessible, quality education;
- to education on attachment to the Moroccan identity and to immutable national constants;
- to professional instruction and to physical and artistic education;
- to decent housing;
- to work and to support of the public authorities in job seeking or self-employment;
- to access to public functions according to merit;
- to access to water and a healthy environment;
- to sustainable development.

Tunisia, Article 40 of the 2014 Constitution.

Work is a right for every citizen, male and female. The State shall take the necessary measures to guarantee work on the basis of competence and fairness.

All citizens, male and female, shall have the right to decent working conditions and to a fair wage.

Chapter 3

The impact of family law on women's economic empowerment in selected MENA countries

The personal status code regulates family matters and domestic relations. This chapter reviews key provisions of the family codes of Algeria, Egypt, Jordan, Libya, Morocco and Tunisia. It examines to what extent these provisions are consonant with the equality and non-discrimination principles set forth in international conventions to which the countries are party and that are incorporated, to varying degrees, into their respective constitutions. The chapter examines women's ability to make autonomous decisions about marriage, the role of male guardians in this context, men's right to have multiple wives and juvenile marriage. It also reviews rights and obligations with respect to family roles and decisions, including the right to work or leave the house. The chapter also puts into perspective gender-based differentiation in relation to wealth, divorce, filiation or heritage.

Introduction

In order to make progress towards gender equality and effectively empower women in their daily lives, standards set by international conventions must be translated into national constitutions and then incorporated into domestic legislative frameworks.

Legislators in the six countries under review have introduced changes to family law that aim to increase equality between men and women, and have worked to align their personal status codes more closely with their international commitments. Morocco, for instance, reformed its family law in 2004, introducing the principle of joint responsibility of spouses in household management; repealing matrimonial tutelage, the obligation of wifely obedience and unilateral divorce at the husband's initiative; and restricting polygamy. Algeria reformed its family law in 2005 to strengthen the status of women within the family, giving equal rights and duties to husbands and wives, requiring husbands to obtain judicial permission to marry subsequent wives and reducing the role of women's male guardians.

Significant discrepancies remain, however, between the levels of equality guaranteed by states' international and constitutional commitments and the provisions in their family laws. Gender-based distinctions persist concerning marriage, family decision making, wealth, divorce, filiation and heritage, with direct and indirect implications for women's autonomy and the rights, obligations and social roles of women and men alike. This inconsistency limits the effectiveness of constitutional reforms aimed at reducing gender-based discrimination, and means that further efforts are needed to eliminate provisions that maintain women and men in inequitable positions. At the same time, it is worth noting that men's high level of responsibility, identified through this review, may also need further examination with a view to achieving greater gender equality.

Whereas the six countries' legal systems are primarily civil, their personal status laws are based to varying degrees on religious interpretations. Discrepancies between the different sets of standards can hinder efforts to close the gender gap.

Box 3.1. **Personal status codes and family law**

"Personal status codes" and "family law" are interchangeable terms that cover concepts adopted by the countries of the MENA region. Imported from French law, where the rules are incorporated into the civil code, the personal status code can be defined as the set of rules that relate directly or indirectly to the life of the family, including inheritance.

The expression "personal status" (*al-ahwal al-shakhsiyya*) is distinct from "real status", which covers property rules (contracts, bonds, etc.). Some countries prefer to use the term "family code" (*qanun al-usra*), but this is equivalent to the personal status code.

Discriminatory personal status laws have negative implications for women's autonomy and adverse effects on their economic security, social roles and self-confidence, which in turn affects their capacity to participate fully in public and economic life. Legislative change on family matters is needed to further women's empowerment, both through full access to the economy and in their personal lives.

Women's autonomy

Laws relating to personal status, marriage and family have an important effect on women's well-being and ability to shape their own lives, including their ability to work. These laws also define men's roles, which have a major bearing on women's autonomy.

As analysed in Chapter 2, the six countries reviewed are parties to the UN Convention on the Elimination of All Forms of Discrimination Against Women (CEDAW). Under the Convention's Article 16.1, States Parties "shall ensure, on a basis of equality of men and women: (a) the same right to enter into marriage; (b) the same right freely to choose a spouse and to enter into marriage only with their free and full consent; (c) the same rights and responsibilities during marriage and at its dissolution."

Women's right to choose whom they marry, what type of marital arrangement they agree to, the timing of their marriage and their age at marriage are critical. Major differences remain among countries on the way women and men are involved in family decision making. These factors affect women's autonomy and agency in both the short term and the longer term, particularly if they are cumulative.

Guardian's consent

One of the cornerstones of autonomy is women's and men's legal capacity to contract their own marriage. Yet a woman's authority to contract her marriage may be restricted through guardianship. A guardian is a person who has the legal authority to care for another person and take decisions for that person, in principle in that person's interest. Men are usually guardians of minors but they may also, in some countries, intervene after the age of majority.

Women in the countries under review remain to various degrees subordinate to men; for example, the term "minor" may be applicable when a woman has reached majority but isn't married. Matrimonial guardianship has been abolished in Morocco and Tunisia. While a woman's consent to her marriage is required in all countries in principle, silence might be considered consent.

- **Jordan**[1] and **Libya**[2] prohibit a woman's marriage without the consent of her guardian (usually her father, or other male relatives in case of death of the father). In Jordan, the guardian's agreement is required for first marriages, meaning that if a divorced woman remarries, she is allowed to sign her marriage contract herself.[3]
- **Egypt** does not require a young woman's guardian to consent to her marriage. Guardianship by the father ends in theory when a child reaches the age of majority (21 years), but for a daughter it normally ends when she gets married or becomes economically independent, even if she is legally an adult.
- In **Algeria**, the guardian's role has become symbolic[4] as he is unable to force a woman to marry against her will or prevent her from marrying whom she chooses. In the event of a conflict with her guardian, the woman can go to court.
- In **Tunisia** and **Morocco** the father is the guardian until a child's majority, but matrimonial guardianship has been abolished.[5]

Polygamy

Polygyny is a form of polygamous marriage under which a man may have more than one wife. In Islam, men are allowed up to four wives at the same time.

In its General Recommendation No. 21 of 1994, the CEDAW Committee denounced polygamy as a violation of the principle of equality between men and women. It said: "States Parties' reports also disclose that polygamy is practiced in a number of countries. Polygamous marriage contravenes a woman's right to equality with men, and can have such serious emotional and financial consequences for her and her dependents that such marriages ought to be discouraged and prohibited. The Committee notes with concern that some States Parties, the constitutions of which guarantee equal rights, permit polygamous marriage in accordance with personal or customary law. This violates the constitutional rights of women, and breaches the provisions of article 5 (a) of the Convention."

Polygamy has been prohibited in **Tunisia** since 1956.[6] In the other five countries under review, legal reforms in recent years have somewhat curtailed men's right to take multiple wives.

- **Morocco,**[7] **Algeria**[8] and **Jordan**[9] have sought to limit polygamy by requiring the prior agreement of a judge. Husbands who wish to marry another wife need to prove that their financial means are sufficient to maintain several marital homes at once. They also have to provide an objective reason to justify their marriage plans (e.g. a man's first wife is sterile and he does not wish to divorce her). **Morocco** requires the first wife's consent, and if she refuses she can file for divorce.[10]
- In **Jordan**[11] and **Egypt**, the first wife or previous wives must be notified of the new marriage. In **Egypt**, the marriage notary is obliged to record the husband's marital status in order to minimise the risk that the husband enters polygamous marriages without the wives' knowledge.[12]
- In **Libya**, the Supreme Court declared in 2013 that restrictions on polygamy, imposed in 1993, were unconstitutional, making polygamy again easily accessible to men.

Discussions with focus groups in the countries under review confirmed that polygamy has a strong impact on women's decision-making power in the family. Sharing the husband's revenue with more than one wife and her children affects not only the financial prospects of women and children but also their psychological well-being. In addition, polygamy makes community of assets difficult during marriage. This practice seems to be more widespread in poorer and rural areas.

Early-age marriage

Marriage at an early age can severely influence women's ability to make independent decisions, including about the family. Being forced to drop out of school before the completion of studies limits women's educational attainment and qualifications for the job market. It has a lifetime impact on their economic opportunities, not to mention the adverse impact that early marriage and pregnancy have on their health.

CEDAW condemns child marriage (Article 16.2): "The betrothal and the marriage of a child shall have no legal effect, and all necessary action, including legislation, shall be taken to specify a minimum age for marriage and to make the registration of marriages in an official registry compulsory." Although the convention does not specify what an acceptable minimum age would be, the CEDAW Committee considered that the minimum age for marriage should be 18 years for both men and women (CEDAW 1994).

All six countries have made strides in raising the minimum age for marriage: it is now 18 years in Egypt,[13] Jordan,[14] Tunisia[15] and Morocco,[16] 19 in Algeria[17] and 20 in Libya.[18] A judicial dispensation can allow a younger woman to be married, except in Egypt, where early age marriage is prohibited in all cases.

According to various studies, a relatively high proportion of women still marry before the minimum age in Egypt, Jordan and Morocco, in particular those in low-income and rural areas (Table 3.1).

Table 3.1. **Marriage rates for girls between 15 and 19 years old**

Libya (1995)	0.9%
Tunisia (2011)	1.2%
Algeria (2008)	2.6%
Jordan (2012)	6.0%
Morocco (2011)	11.0%
Egypt (2014)	14.7%

Source: United Nations, Department of Economic and Social Affairs, Population Division (2015), *World Marriage Data* 2015 (POP/DB/Marr/Rev2015), www.un.org/en/development/desa/population/theme/marriage-unions/WMD2015.shtml.

The marriage rate of minors is high in Egypt, even though the practice is legally banned. Such marriages remain unregistered and not recognised by the law, which raises questions about the protection of the wife's rights. Furthermore, a provision introduced in 2000 makes divorce from these unauthorised marriages possible, in effect giving de facto recognition to the practice.

Guardianship by men over women and their involvement in decisions about a woman's marriage, as well as polygyny and early marriages, stunt women's autonomy and freedom to choose how and with whom to live their lives. These conditions affect their capacity to shape their own destinies, economic and otherwise, free from coercion.

The marriage contract

In the six countries under review, financial conditions are set prior to marriage during intense prenuptial negotiations between the two spouses' families. The dowry is a payment by the future husband to the bride that becomes her legal property at the time of marriage. Negotiations focus on the amount of the dowry and the respective contribution of the two families towards the couple's future home and furnishings. A portion of the dowry is paid at the signing of the marriage contract and the remainder, often a larger share, is paid to support the wife in the event of a marriage termination (divorce or the husband's death). Neither the bride's parents nor her husband have legal claims to the dowry (see below on property rights and ownership of marital assets).

The family laws in all six countries allow the spouses to add conditions to the marriage contract. In theory both the bride and the groom may write such conditions, but in practice only the bride needs to do so, in order to increase her rights (Quarischi and Vogel, 2008: 201). She may negotiate the inclusion of contractual clauses, such as her right to leave the couple's home or to engage in a profession. Failure to abide by these stipulations is grounds for divorce.

In Algeria, Morocco and Tunisia, the principle of obedience was abrogated and joint responsibility was adopted (see below on decision making), making this type of clause unnecessary; however, it might still be in interest of the wife. In Egypt, Jordan and Libya, where the husband can end financial maintenance of the wife on the grounds that he did not authorise her to leave the house or work, the insertion of a clause in the marriage contract enables the wife to continue her education, seek employment or travel abroad without having to ask permission.

In practice, the right to include special clauses in a marriage contract is not often exercised. Discussions with focus groups highlighted that the future bride rarely demands clauses such as the right to work. Women are often not aware of their rights and, even when they are, strong social pressure dissuades future brides from mentioning this issue during prenuptial negotiations. Also, civil service officers who meet with the engaged couple – and these officers are almost always men – tend to show little enthusiasm for such clauses and often do not mention the possibility of including them. Even when a bride manages to have these clauses included, it often takes several years of court proceedings to ensure their application and to punish any violation.

Focus group discussions underscored that the legal guarantees provided in a marriage contract are not always respected due to entrenched social perceptions. A woman going out to work may be viewed as a proof that her husband cannot bear the household expenses alone. Criticism from family, neighbours and society can lead husbands in Jordan to prohibit their wives from working outside the home.

In Egypt, focus group participants indicated that mentalities are gradually changing, with certain husbands encouraging their wives to work and contribute to the financial costs of the household. In the lower strata of society, though, a woman who works before marriage may reduce her chances of finding a husband, as it is considered a sign of poverty and her need for financial resources. Women from the lowest social classes often work to buy their *trousseau* and then withdraw from the labour market after marriage (El-Kholy, 2002).

Decision making: reciprocity versus duty to obey

The role and place a woman occupies in the family affects her ability to think and act within as well as outside the household.

Under CEDAW's Article 16.1, States Parties should ensure that men and women have "the same rights and responsibilities during marriage and at its dissolution" and "the same personal rights as husband and wife, including the right to choose a family name, a profession and an occupation".

Personal status laws in the six countries define women's agency within the family differently. Several countries have revoked the principle of women's obedience, while others maintain it.

- **Egypt** and **Jordan** support the notion of a wife's duty to obey in exchange for her right to financial maintenance. This means that a husband can stop maintaining his wife if he considers that she was disobedient and left the house without permission[19] or if he can prove that her work is detrimental to the family's interests.[20] In Jordan, however, a husband who has given explicit consent in the marriage contract to his wife's employment, or tacit consent, for example if the wife was working before the marriage,[21] may not revoke consent without legitimate evidence that he has suffered harm.[22]

- In **Libya**, the law does not mention a wife's duty of obedience, but she has the right to expect her husband to provide maintenance and associated expenses within the limits of his means.[23] The husband also has the right to expect his wife to provide maintenance and associated expenses if she has the means and he does not.[24] In all cases, the husband is in charge of supervising the home.[25]
- **Algeria**, **Morocco** and **Tunisia** have abrogated the principle of wifely obedience and instituted reciprocal spousal duties (Tunisia, Algeria) or joint responsibility (Morocco) (Box 3.2).

Box 3.2. **Reciprocity or joint family responsibility**

Tunisia: Reciprocal duties of spouses

In 1993, Tunisia replaced the wife's duty to obey with the reciprocal duty of both spouses to treat each other kindly, to maintain good relations and to avoid causing injury to the other.[1] Spouses shall co-operate in the management of family affairs, the proper education of their children and the conduct of their children's affairs, including education, travel and financial transactions.[2] The law thus establishes complementarity and independence as the new basis for relations between spouses.

In 2000, Tunisia abolished the provision in the Code of Obligations and Contracts that made the validity of a work contract concluded by the wife subject to the husband's authorisation and gave the husband the right to break an engagement concluded without his assent.[3]

Morocco: Joint responsibility of spouses and right of women to undertake a trade

In 2004, Morocco adopted the principle of joint responsibility for spouses in the management of the family.[4] Both spouses are responsible for managing the family and bringing up the children, and a wife with financial resources must contribute towards providing for the needs of the family.

Spouses have reciprocal rights and duties:[5]

- legal cohabitation, which includes marital obligations and relationships, justice and equity in case of polygamy, kindness and dedication to each other, an obligation of fidelity, protection of honour and procreation;
- marital relations with mutual respect, compassion and mercy, and preservation of the best interest of the family;
- joint responsibility in the overall household management and children's upbringing;
- mutual consultation in decision making related to management of the household, as well as children's affairs and family planning;
- due respect and kindness to each spouse's relatives, visiting and inviting them over;
- the right of inheritance between the two (Article 51).

The Code of Commerce of 1996 (Article 17) expressly authorises married women to exercise a trade without the husband's authorisation. Any agreement to the contrary is deemed null and void.

Box 3.2. **Reciprocity or joint family responsibility** *(continued)*

Algeria: Reciprocal obligations of spouses

In 2005, Algeria abolished the wife's duty of obedience and replaced it by a series of reciprocal rights and duties of the husband and wife:[6]

- To preserve conjugal ties and the duties of life together;
- To cohabitate in harmony, mutual respect and kindness;
- To contribute jointly to the preservation of the family's interests, the protection of their children, and the provision of a sound education for them;
- To ensure mutual agreement in the management of the family's affairs, and the spacing of births;
- To respect their respective parents and other family members, and visit them;
- To preserve the ties of kinship and good relations with parents and other family members;
- To enjoy the right to visit and receive visits from parents and other family members in kindness.

A husband who exerts pressure on his wife to dispose of her assets or her financial resources risks a prison term of six months to two years.

Notes:

1. Article 23 of the 1956 Tunisian Personal Status Law as amended in 1993.
2. Ibid.
3. Law no. 2000-17 of 7 February 2000.
4. Article 4 of the 2004 Moroccan Family Law.
5. Article 51 of the 2004 Moroccan Family Law.
6. Article 36 of the 2005 Algerian Family Law.

Source: Author's own research based on countries' national laws.

The emergence of standards of joint responsibility and reciprocity represents a change in both men's and women's rights but not necessarily in their roles. Thus in Tunisia, both spouses must fulfil their conjugal duties "in accordance with custom and usual practices" and "the husband, as head of the family, must support the needs of the spouse and the children within his capabilities and in accordance with their status in the context of maintenance payments. The wife must contribute to family expenses if she has the means."[26] Such explicit provisions on differences between the husband's and wife's contributions are not made in Algeria and Morocco.

Hence, although the spouses have the duty to collaborate, the husband has a duty to maintain the wife. While the woman should have a certain autonomy in her decision making and ability to work, the change may not immediately affect social behaviours (Box 3.3).

Legal provisions towards more equality and women's rights seem not to have adequately modified the traditional gender divide. Women continue to assume the bulk of domestic chores, which can be an impediment to their engaging in a full-time work over a long period.

Box 3.3. **Traditional women's duties**

Changes introduced in the family codes may not induce immediate changes in the traditional, patriarchal perceptions according to which the husband is the head of the household who will provide for the family and who is responsible for the children. Such notions dictate the home as the proper sphere for women's participation. "Even when a woman, driven by economic necessity, succeeds in obtaining a wage-paying job, she, in many cases, receives no real, substantial assistance from the man with housework. Nor does her employment allow her to fulfil herself in that it is meant only to help raise the family's standard of living." (UNDP, 2006: 168).

Household tasks may limit women's access to the labour market. The stress of balancing family life with paid employment may dissuade them from looking for a job and encourage them to stay at home; it may also lead them to withdraw from professional life.

In Algeria, Morocco and Tunisia, time-use surveys show that all categories of women devote about seven times more time per day than men to unpaid work, carrying out domestic chores and looking after children, elderly people or dependents living at home with them (EBRD, 2015).

The heavy burden of domestic responsibilities often leads women to leave the labour market when they marry and have children; this is an oft-cited cause of the pattern of workforce participation in the MENA region (see Chapter 1, Figure 1.5). The trend is reinforced when a wife has to ask her husband for permission to work outside the home. This general behavioural pattern limits the employment of women, whose professional occupation may be viewed as "optional" vis-à-vis men's duty to be the breadwinner. This factor, in turn, may contribute to an increase in women's unemployment relative to men's.

Property rights and ownership of marital assets

Under CEDAW's Article 16.1(h), States Parties shall ensure "the same rights for both spouses in respect of the ownership, acquisition, management, administration, enjoyment and disposition of property, whether free of charge or for a valuable consideration."

In the six countries, the default matrimonial regime is separation of property. Each spouse retains individual ownership of assets brought into the marriage, and assets obtained during the marriage are registered in their individual names. Women and men have equal rights to acquire, manage and own their property. If the wife has assets of her own upon her marriage, she can subsequently administer and manage them freely and independently. The Tunisian personal status code states expressly that the husband has no administrative power over his wife's assets.[27]

Despite these provisions, women's financial security remains limited in practice. First, the wife often has very limited or no assets. Then, throughout the marriage, property, including the family home, is usually registered in the husband's name.

As highlighted by the focus groups, although women are not responsible for the financial upkeep of their household, most working women contribute to household expenses (in Jordan they give their income to their father if they are not married). Since assets purchased are usually registered in the husband's name, the wife has no rights to them under the regulations on the separation of marital assets.

Enabling women to own property jointly with their spouses would increase their access to and control over marital economic assets, thereby improving their financial stability and security. It would also strengthen their ability to engage economically, in particular in entrepreneurial activities, as it would facilitate women's access to credit by providing the required collateral more easily (see the discussion of access to finance below). Finally, it would increase their assets in the case of divorce or the husband's death.

All six countries have introduced the possibility of sharing assets. Tunisia introduced an optional matrimonial property regime of communal assets in 1998, which the spouses may adopt at the time of marriage or thereafter. Morocco and Algeria also introduced the possibility of joint ownership, in 2004 and 2005 respectively. In Morocco spouses may make such an agreement in writing in a document separate from the marriage contract.[28] In Algeria, a clause can be included in the marriage contract, or the community of assets can be established later in a separate document.[29] In Egypt, Libya and Jordan, spouses may also opt for communal assets in the marriage contract.

The focus groups indicated that, in practice, few spouses opt for joint-title matrimonial agreements. In Jordan the portion of assets registered in the names of both spouses seems to be increasing somewhat.

Freedom of movement

Freedom of movement is an indispensable condition for women's ability to participate in economic life. It allows them access to markets, employment, business activities and services. Limited geographic mobility can be a barrier on women's capacity to work, especially in high-responsibility positions for which they may need to travel.

Freedom of movement is enshrined in CEDAW (Article 15.4): "States Parties shall accord to men and women the same rights with regard to the law relating to the movement of persons and the freedom to choose their residence and domicile." The constitutions of all six countries are in conformity with CEDAW and guarantee freedom of movement.[30] In principle, all citizens enjoy the right to move freely and to choose their place of residence within the territory of a state and their right to leave the country.

However, women still suffer from restrictions on their mobility, established by a range of national laws and by family control over their choices. Freedom of movement is influenced by marital status, age and work status.

- In **Jordan**, fathers (or guardians) can decide on a daughter's travel and place of residence as well as her type of education until the age of 30, and this right is extended if a daughter is considered "untrustworthy" by court order.
- In **Egypt** and **Jordan**, the wife's duty to obey may restrict her freedom of movement, in particular her right to leave the couple's home and travel abroad. It thus may stand in the way of a woman's access to employment or ability to set up a business. Until 2009, Jordan's reservation to Article 15(4) stated that the wife's residence was with her husband. In Egypt (2000)[31] and Jordan (2013),[32] laws have been amended that required the husband to give his consent before his wife could be issued a passport and travel abroad.
- **Algeria** and **Morocco** have not lifted their reservation to Article 15(4).
- In **Libya**, although the obligation of obedience is not mentioned as such in the law,[33] courts consider that a wife who goes out, works or travels without a

husband's permission has committed wrongdoing, justifying a husband's right to divorce unilaterally without payment of any financial compensation.

- **Tunisian** courts have introduced an obligation for the wife to cohabit with her husband at a domicile chosen by the latter. This notion may influence women's movements and, as a result, their professional opportunities.

The focus groups noted that in practice the husband does sometimes manage to prevent his wife from leaving the country by confiscating her passport or giving her name to immigration authorities in order to prevent her from going abroad, especially when travelling with her children.[34] Strong social norms also incite women to ask their husband's permission to travel abroad, even when such permission is not legally necessary. In a 2011 study including Morocco (EBRD, 2015: 85), single and young women reported feeling partly or completely restricted from leaving the house without permission. Women in paid work, elderly married women or divorced women are freer to leave the house without permission.

Women's mobility is furthermore influenced by the quality and security of transportation systems. Poor infrastructure and shortcomings in transportation arrangements, coupled with a lack of security and frequent violence in public spaces (and the workplace), have a major impact on women's economic participation. Lower geographical mobility restricts job choices and negatively affects women's earnings.

Overall, progress towards equality in the constitutions of Algeria, Morocco, Tunisia and Libya is to some extent reflected in their family law provisions, where women's duty to obey has been abrogated and replaced by the principle of reciprocal duties or joint responsibility. This change runs through other provisions where attention has been given to enhancing equality, including through the abrogation of matrimonial guardianship and the banning or limiting of polygamy. In Egypt and Jordan, however, the principle of obedience of the wife has not yet been revoked, despite the equality principle set by the constitution, and the concept of guardianship is active in Jordan. Overall, the traditional approach towards gender roles – with men as the breadwinners and heads of households, and women tasked with household chores and childcare – still seems to dominate, with consequences for women's autonomy and empowerment to act according to their own choices.

Dissolution of marriage

CEDAW's Article 16.1(c) calls for States Parties to ensure that men and women have the same rights and responsibilities in the event of dissolution of marriage.

Some progress has been made towards greater equality between women and men in the right to ask for divorce, in particular in Tunisia, Algeria and Morocco. In the other countries, divorce procedures are still easier for men. In many cases, the financial consequences of the dissolution of marriage weaken women's economic and social status. Also, even if the mother has custody of the children, the father maintains authority as guardian over the most important decisions.

Ability to initiate a divorce

The conditions under which men and women can divorce still depend on gender. A husband's right unilaterally to divorce his wife still exists in Egypt, Jordan and Libya, while the provisions under which women can initiate a divorce must be submitted to a judge in all cases. Also, the financial consequences of a divorce are often detrimental to women.

- In **Tunisia** (1956)[35] and **Morocco** (2004),[36] men and women have equal rights to initiate the dissolution of the marriage. Procedures can be initiated on the grounds of unilateral will, fault or mutual consent. The divorce is to be pronounced by a judge, and unilateral repudiation is prohibited.
- In **Algeria,**[37] a husband who wishes to terminate a marriage must address a judge, who cannot refuse to register the dissolution of the marriage but will attempt reconciliation between the two spouses. The judge may also require the husband to pay financial compensation to his spouse if the dissolution is deemed abusive.
- **Egypt,**[38] **Jordan**[39] and **Libya** maintain the husband's power to repudiate a wife, i.e. to dissolve the marriage unilaterally without any justification and without the spouse's presence; the husband need only appear before a marriage civil servant and register his wish to dissolve the union. If the repudiation is pronounced orally, it is the wife who must go to court to have the divorce registered.

Unilateral divorce by the husband weakens women substantially and acts as a permanent threat to their well-being and social status. With no right to compensation, her household income falls significantly and she becomes dependent on her family or social welfare, where it is available. For fear of repudiation, women often dare not oppose a spouse hostile to any of their actions, including employment.

In all six countries, the wife may file for fault-based divorce but she must convince the court that she has suffered prejudice, and the legal proceedings may be lengthy, complex, tense and costly.

In **Algeria,**[40] **Egypt,**[41] **Jordan,**[43] **Libya**[43]and **Morocco,**[44] women may file for *khul'* in court. *Khul'* is a procedure of unilateral cessation of marriage on the initiative of the wife, who does not have to prove the fault of her husband. It implies that she gives compensation to her husband, the amount of which is generally determined by the courts. In Egypt, she renounces all of her financial interests and returns her dowry. For Egyptian women who can afford to return the dowry, the procedure is easier than fault-based divorce; in the case of poor women, the value of the dowry is quite low, but a woman may be rather dependent on the dowry and it may be difficult for her to give it back.

In the six countries, the husband is required to pay alimony during "*idda*", the mandatory waiting period before a divorce becomes effective (three months in Algeria,[45] Egypt, Jordan,[46] Tunisia[47] and Libya;[48] four months and ten days in Morocco[49]). The waiting period is intended to ascertain that the wife is not pregnant by her husband.[50] After this period, he is no longer required by law to maintain his former wife.

Upon termination of the marriage, the wife will usually receive the part of her dowry that was not paid to her when the couple married. If she does not bear responsibility for the separation, she will also receive compensation in the six countries analysed.[51] The judge determines the amount, based on the duration of the marriage and the husband's financial means. It may be paid in one lump sum or in several monthly payments. According to sources in the region, husbands sometimes seek to portray themselves as owning very little personal wealth or having reduced income in order to limit payments.

The economic and social consequences of a divorce are frequently harsh for women, who are often stigmatised. Moreover, as mentioned above, due to the separation of property, divorce may impose severe financial penalties on women, in particular those who have no personal wealth. The wife has no right to the assets acquired during the marriage, including the family home, if these assets are registered in her husband's name, even after a long married life and even if she contributed to their acquisition either directly, for instance by reimbursing a loan, or indirectly through her work in the household. In Tunisia, the optional regime of communal assets seeks to "ensure that the spouses have joint ownership of any property or group of properties which are specifically intended for the family's use". In the event of divorce, property assets acquired after the wedding date will be shared between the spouses.

The *khul'* is believed to have strengthened women's power of negotiation in the marital home, providing them with leverage to insist that their husband allow them to work. Studies suggest that it triggered a substantial increase in the rate of female employment, particularly in the 24-35 age bracket, between 1980 and 2008 in the MENA countries where it was introduced. Faced with the possibility that their marriage could end in divorce, women sought to obtain paid employment, enabling them to be independent in the event of the breakdown of their marital union (Hassani and Sjögren, 2014).

Children's guardianship and custody

CEDAW's Article 16.1 provides for equal rights between mothers and fathers in matters relating to their children. It enjoins States Parties to ensure, on a basis of equality between men and women, "the same rights and responsibilities as parents, irrespective of their marital status, in matters relating to their children" (16.1(d)) and "the same rights and responsibilities with regard to guardianship, wardship, trusteeship and adoption of children, or similar institutions where these concepts exist in national legislation" (16.1(f)), adding in both clauses that "in all cases the interests of the children shall be paramount."

Yet women and men in the six countries under review do not have equal rights over their children, including upon dissolution of marriage. The husband is in general the legal guardian of his minor children during the marriage and in the event of its dissolution. The mother may retain custody of her children until they reach a certain age but, depending on the country, she will have to defer to the father in all or most decisions under the guardianship principle.

- In **Tunisia**, since 1993, if custody is granted to the mother in the event of divorce, she shall enjoy the prerogatives of guardianship with respect to the travel and education of the children and management of their financial accounts.[52] However, the father maintains guardianship for all other matters unless he dies or a judge declares him unable,[53] in which case guardianship is attributed to the mother. As custodian of the child and despite some rights to act as guardian over certain decisions in case of divorce, the mother must keep a reasonable distance from the guardian to enable him to fulfil his duties, or she may lose custody.[54] This may prevent divorced women from accepting work opportunities in another city for fear they may lose custody of their children.
- In **Algeria**, the father is usually the guardian of the child.[55] The mother can replace the father as legal guardian in emergency situations, for instance when he is absent or unable to act as guardian.[56] Guardianship is transferred to the mother if the father dies.[57] In case of divorce and since 2005, work cannot be a sufficient reason for depriving a mother of her right of custody[58] and the parent who is granted custody is also given the right of guardianship.[59] A woman who remarries loses custody of her children.[60]
- In **Morocco** the father is the legal guardian,[61] and in the event of divorce the mother needs to involve him in all administrative and legal acts relating to the

child. Hence, insurance companies, for instance, systematically reimburse the father for medical expenses incurred due to a minor child's illness or accident, even if the mother has paid the bills. The father is also considered to be in charge of a child's bank account even if the mother opened and manages it. Guardianship may be awarded to the mother in cases of incapacity of the father.[62] A woman who remarries loses custody, except in some exceptional circumstances.[63]

- In **Egypt** and **Jordan**, in the event of divorce, the father must pay alimony until the child reaches adulthood. In Egypt, this obligation extends until a son completes his studies or until the marriage or financial independence of a daughter.[64] In exchange, the father exercises guardianship over property and persons, and performs administrative procedures concerning the children on his own (management of bank accounts even if supplied by the mother; choice of education system, educational institution, professional orientation; authorisation to undergo medical treatment; obtaining an identity card and passport, etc.). In the event of the death or incapacity of the father, guardianship is awarded to the closest male relative.[65] A woman who remarries in Jordan may, depending on the judge, lose custody of the children. In Egypt, a woman who remarries loses custody. This is not stated directly in Egyptian law; rather it became a common legal practice pursuant to a key Court of Cassation decision, Case No. 75 Judicial Year 53, 19 March 1985 (ruling available on the legal database Mohamoon).[66]
- In **Libya**, custody is transmitted to the mother after divorce, but she gets guardianship of her children only if the father dies or upon a court decision.[67]

Focus group participants noted that a woman's ability to dissolve an unsatisfactory marriage is hindered by the economic, social and emotional effects of divorce. For example, a divorce may affect her housing. If a couple has children, the mother will in principle be able to live with them in the home for the time of the custody. Under Tunisia's personal status code, the father grants the residence of the custodial mother.[68] If the woman has no children or is not the custodian, however, she may have to return to her parents' home if she does not have sufficient financial means to pay for her own housing.

And while a court judgment usually requires the husband to pay monthly maintenance to the children's mother until they come of age if she is the custodian, in practice many former husbands do not respect the alimony ruling, and women without any other source of revenue can thus end up in extremely precarious situations. Courts are swamped with claims from divorced women for the payment of alimony. As enforcement of court decisions is difficult, Algeria, Egypt, Jordan, Morocco and Tunisia introduced a guarantee fund to which divorced women can turn to obtain funding.

Reforms of provisions governing the dissolution of marriage have sought to introduce greater equality, though men and women do not have the same rights and in none of the six countries do women and men enjoy equal rights. Morocco and Tunisia provide that both spouses can initiate the dissolution of the marriage for the same reasons and according to the same procedure, but financial outcomes vary by gender. In the other four countries, differences on the divorce procedure remain. Moreover, none of the countries offers equality in guardianship and head-of-household provisions or in the financial arrangements that apply to childcare in the case of divorce.

In light of their often precarious financial situation following a divorce, many women are forced to join the workforce in poor conditions. They often join the informal sector, especially if they lack prior work experience, and may have to accept low-paid, strenuous work with no social protection.

Box 3.4. **The family book in Jordan**

An official family book (*daftar al-a'ilah*) is needed in Jordan for a large number of administrative procedures, including voting, running for elected office, accessing social services, applying for personal documents, registering children for school, and employment in the public sector. Before marriage, a woman remains in the family book of her father or another male relative where guardianship is recorded; after marriage she is transferred to the family book of her husband.

A divorced or widowed woman can now start and maintain her own family book, but she cannot include her children. In the event of divorce, children remain in the family book of their father. A widow's children are placed in the family book of their male guardian, normally a male relative of the deceased husband. These measures exclude mothers from decision making on the welfare of their children.

Sources: World Bank (2013), *Hashemite Kingdom of Jordan: Jordan Country Gender Assessment: Economic Participation, Agency and Access to Justice in Jordan,* Washington, DC. http://documents.worldbank.org/curated/en/503361468038992583/pdf/ACS51580WP0P130ox0379850B00PUBLIC0.pdf; World Bank (2013), *Opening Doors: Gender Equality and Development in the Middle East and North Africa*, World Bank, Washington, DC. https://openknowledge.worldbank.org/handle/10986/12552.

Inequality in inheritance rights

Denying women equal inheritance rights violates the non-discrimination principle embodied in CEDAW and is detrimental to their economic security and development.

The CEDAW Committee has declared that men and women with the same degree of relationship to a deceased person should be entitled to equal shares in the estate: "There are many countries where the law and practice concerning inheritance and property result in serious discrimination against women. As a result of this uneven treatment, women may receive a smaller share of the husband's or father's property at his death than would widowers and sons. In some instances, women are granted limited and controlled rights and receive income only from the deceased's property. Often inheritance rights for widows do not reflect the principles of equal ownership of property acquired during marriage. Such provisions contravene the Convention and should be abolished." (CEDAW, 1994).

Existing inheritance legislation in the six countries remains discriminatory along gender lines. Each heir receives a specific share of the inheritance in accordance with that person's kinship to the deceased – and in general female heirs are entitled to only half the share to which men are entitled. A widow will receive one-eighth of her deceased husband's assets or one-fourth if he has no children.

The Tunisian code of personal status establishes that "the male heir receives twice as much inheritance as a female heir."[69] The other five states apply the same rule.[70] This inequality is based on the rationale that men have a greater need for assets, as it is their responsibility to maintain their family in a broad sense (including notably widowed or unmarried mothers and sisters), whereas women have no such financial obligations.

The focus groups indicated that customs and traditions can further hamper women's access to an inheritance. For example, it is not uncommon for the family to pressure female heirs into relinquishing their full inheritance rights in favour of male relatives. Many women do not know that they can refuse to cede their rights or can appeal to the courts. They may also renounce asking for their rights for fear of reprisals and to avoid stigma from their family and society.

Jordan has taken steps to help women avoid waiving rights to their full inheritance. Heirs must register their inheritance, and all transactions involving a transfer of property rights is forbidden during three months following the death of the testator (Box. 3.5).

Box 3.5. **Good practice of inheritance rules in Jordan**

Jordan introduced a regulation in 2010 that tightened the procedure for waiving the right to a portion of an inheritance (Article 319 of the 2010 Jordanian Personal Status Law grants the Office of the Chief Justice the right to issue procedural regulations). This regulation obliges all heirs to register their immovable inheritance in their name and prohibits any transactions involving a transfer of inheritance rights until three months after the death of the testator.

"This regulation is designed to ensure that the person is made aware of his or her rights, to ensure transparency and to thereby prevent the waiver from being given immediately after the death of the testator, as used to happen in the past. Several governmental and civil society organisations are actively involved in raising awareness of the relevant legislation and they provide legal advice in this regard" (CEDAW, 2012).

The regulation enables female heirs to escape pressure from relatives to renounce their inheritance rights and gives them time to evaluate their options before taking a decision. Such a procedure could ensure women greater access to financial assets.

While this practice may prove positive, it must be noted that to ensure that land remains in the father's family, especially in rural regions, women are sometimes excluded from their inheritance on the grounds that they are not named as potential heirs. Land may also be divided among male heirs before the father dies, as it is possible to make living bequests and donations. Women are then put under pressure not to claim their share. Bequests and donations can also be used positively to ensure that wives, daughters and sisters receive a higher share of assets than foreseen in the legal provisions on inheritance.

- **Tunisia**, which allows for the community of assets, tries to encourage lifetime bequests between spouses, between parents and their children, and between brothers and sisters by lowering the registration taxes and stamp duties in comparison to other types of bequests.[71] Under a 2006 law, donations between ascendants and descendants and between spouses are exempt from the donation tax. It is also possible for a testator to transfer assets through a will, although this method is limited to one-third of the assets.[72]
- In **Egypt**, the heirs may conclude an agreement among themselves to the effect that the inheritance will be divided into equal parts between males and females. Some families transfer assets to their daughters during their lifetime. Others reach agreements that all assets will be divided equally between sisters and brothers. This is not a common practice, however, particularly in rural areas.

A woman's access to an inheritance and receipt of an equal share have a significant impact on her financial security. With a limited inheritance, women can end up without sufficient assets or resources to support themselves. For example, if a wife has no personal assets, she may find herself destitute and deprived of the marital home unless she has minor children in her care.

Box 3.6. **How equality in inheritance can improve outcomes for girls: a case study in India**

A reform of inheritance rights in two states in India shows that giving women greater access to assets through inheritance can change outcomes for children, particularly girls.

In 1994, the states of Karnataka and Maharashtra reformed the Hindu Succession Act to allow women and men the same rights to inherit joint family property. This altered control over assets within families and increased parental investments in daughters. The second-generation effects were even larger in areas such as the education of daughters. For example, mothers who benefited from the reform spent twice as much on their daughters' education. Moreover, where the reforms occurred, women were more likely to have bank accounts and their households were more likely to have sanitary latrines. The reforms suggest that legal empowerment gives women more bargaining power within the household and leads to better educational and financial outcomes.

Source: World Bank (2016), *Women, Business and the Law,* World Bank, Washington, DC. http://wbl.worldbank.org/~/media/WBG/WBL/Documents/Reports/2016/Women-Business-and-the-Law-2016.pdf.

Conclusions

Inequalities in matters of marriage, family decision making, property rights, freedom of movement, divorce and inheritance have consequences on women's personal, psychological and financial security. This affects their autonomy and empowerment to make their own choices.

Some progress has been made in the six countries towards increasing equality between women and men. The abrogation in some countries of women's obligation to obedience should be acknowledged, as should introduction of the principle of mutual consent to, and reciprocity in, marriage. Laws regulating polygamy and divorce have also been changed.

Yet key inequalities remain on marriage, family decision making and divorce. Family law provisions are not yet in conformity with the countries' international commitments to equality and with provisions included in their constitutions. Women and men still have unequal capacities to exercise agency in the family, and current provisions constrain women's autonomy, in particular when they must obtain authorisation to work from their husbands or fathers. Limits on women's property rights and assets also represent a considerable barrier to their economic development. As was stressed during discussions in focus groups, reforms have not yet translated into new social norms, and this also limits women's participation in the economy.

Recommendations

Governments are encouraged to:

- Ensure that family law is in line with the principles outlined in international commitments and the country's constitution, and in particular that the personal status code is harmonised with the principle of gender equality and does not include provisions that are discriminatory in nature.

- Ensure an equitable distribution of duties between spouses and include a woman's right to work and travel without her husband's consent in legislative texts and/or promote the opportunity for women to include beneficial clauses in their marriage contract, such as the right to work and travel.
- Support the application of community property between spouses and allow women equal rights to assets acquired during the marriage in the event of divorce.
- Reconsider inheritance laws to ensure gender equality and encourage bequests between spouses or between parents and their heirs and follow Jordan's example and freeze a woman's share of the inheritance so that she is protected from being forced to renounce her inheritance rights.
- Raise awareness of the hardships women face within the current structures, in particular in the case of divorce, and improve their protection and rights, for instance allowing mothers to hold the status of "head of the family" or improve enforcement mechanisms.
- Create an expert task force to examine the economic impact of family law provisions, and develop recommendations on legal reforms that would help women engage more in the economic sphere. The task force could also examine whether and how men's high level of responsibility could negatively impact countries' competitiveness.

Notes

1. Article 14 of the 2010 Jordanian Personal Status Law.
2. Article 7 of the 1984 Libyan Personal Status Law.
3. Article 19 of the 2010 Jordanian Personal Status Law.
4. Article 11 of the 2005 Algerian Family Law.
5. Articles 24 and 25 of the 2004 Moroccan Family Law.
6. Article 18 of the 1956 Tunisian Personal Status Law.
7. Articles 40-46 of the 2004 Moroccan Family Law.
8. Article 8 of 2005 Algerian Family Law.
9. Article 13 of the 2010 Jordanian Personal Status Law.
10. Article 45 of the 2004 Moroccan Family Law.
11. Article 13 of the 2010 Jordanian Personal Status Law.
12. Article 11 bis of Egypt's Law No. 25/1929, as amended through Law No. 100/1985.
13. Article 31 bis of Egypt's 1993 Child Law, as amended in 2008.
14. Article 10 of the 2010 Jordanian Personal Status Law.
15. Law of 2007, amending some provisions of the 1956 Tunisian Personal Status Law.
16. Article 19 of the 2004 Moroccan Family Law. It is also 18 years for men.
17. Article 7 of the 2005 Algerian Family Law.
18. Article 6 of the 1984 Libyan Personal Status Law. It is also 20 years for men.

19. See, for instance, Article 62 of the Jordanian 2010 Personal Status Law.
20. Article 1 para. 4 of the 1920 Egyptian Law, as amended in 1985.
21. This is the courts' interpretation in accommodating the duty to obey versus the right to work.
22. CEDAW (2015), Sixth periodic report of States Parties due in 2016 (Jordan), p. 50, 25 June 2015, http://tbinternet.ohchr.org/_layouts/treatybodyexternal/Download.aspx?symbolno=CEDAW%2fC%2fJOR%2f6&Lang=en.
23. Article 17 of the 1984 Libyan Personal Status Law.
24. Article 18 of the 1984 Libyan Personal Status Law.
25. Ibid.
26. Article 23 of the1956 Tunisian Personal Status Law, as amended in 1993. Former Article 23 required a wife to obey her husband and to "perform her conjugal duties in accordance with usage and custom".
27. Article 24 of the 1956 Tunisian Personal Status Law.
28. Article 49 of the 2004 Moroccan Family Law.
29. Article 37 of the 2005 Algerian Family Law.
30. Article 55 of the 2016 Algerian Constitution, Article 62 of the 2014 Egyptian Constitution, Article 9 of the 1952 Jordanian Constitution, Article 24 of the 2011 Libyan Transitional Constitution, Article 24 of the 2011 Moroccan Constitution, Article 25 of the 2014 Tunisian Constitution.
31. In November 2000, the Supreme Constitutional Court ruled unconstitutional Article 3 of a 1996 decree requiring the husband's approval for the delivery of a passport to a married woman.
32. Article 12 of the Temporary Passports Law, which made the issuance of a wife's passport conditional upon the agreement of her husband or guardian, was removed.
33. Cancelled under Article 73 of the 1984 Libyan Personal Status Law.
34. Since November 2015, a Tunisian mother can apply for her children's passports and no longer must present the father's travel authorisation to airport police when she leaves the country (Law of 10 November 2015 amending and completing the Law of 1975 concerning passports and travel documents).
35. Article 30 of the1956 Tunisian Personal Status Law.
36. Articles 78-93 of the 1984 Libyan Personal Status Law, as amended in 2005.
37. Article 52 of the 2005 Algerian Family Law.
38. Article 5 bis of the 1929 Law, as amended in 1985.
39. Articles 80 and 97 of the 2010 Jordan Personal Status Law.
40. Article 54 of the 2005 Algerian Family Law.
41. Article 20 of the 2000 Law.
42. Articles 103-109 of the 2010 Jordanian Personal Status Law.
43. Articles 29-45 of the 1984 Libyan Personal Status Law.
44. Articles 115-120 of the 2004 Moroccan Family Law.
45. Article 58 of the 2005 Algerian Family Law.
46. Article 147 of the 2010 Jordanian Personal Status Law.
47. Articles 35 and 38 of the 1956 Tunisian Personal Status Law.
48. Article 52 of the 1984 Libyan Personal Status Law.
49. Article 132 of the 2004 Moroccan Family Law.

50. Esposito, J.L and N. DeLong-Bas (2001), *Women in Muslim Family Law*, Syracuse University Press, p. 79.
51. Egypt: Article 16 and 17 para. 1 of the 1929 Law as amended 1985; Jordan: Article 155 of the 2010 Jordanian Personal Status Law; Algeria: Articles 52 and 53 bis of the 2005 Algerian Family Law; Libya: Article 51 of the 1984 Libyan Personal Status Law; Tunisia: Article 31 of the 1956 Tunisian Personal Status Law; Morocco: Article 101 of the 2004 Moroccan Family Law.
52. Article 67 of the 1956 Tunisian Personal Status Law, as amended in 1993.
53. Article 154 of the 1956 Tunisian Personal Status Law, as amended in 1981.
54. Article 61 of the 1956 Tunisian Personal Status Law.
55. Article 87 of the 2005 Algerian Family Code.
56. Article 87 of the 2005 Algerian Family Law.
57. Article 87 of the 2005 Algerian Family Law.
58. Article 67 of the 2005 Algerian Family Law.
59. Article 87 of the 2005 Algerian Family Law.
60. Article 66 of the 2005 Algerian Family Law.
61. Article 236 of the 2004 Moroccan Family Law.
62. Article 231 of the 2004 Moroccan Family Law.
63. Article 175 of the 2004 Moroccan Family Law.
64. Article 18 bis2 of the 1920 Law as amended in 1985.
65. Article 28 of the 1952 Egyptian Law Decree and Article 223 of the Jordanian 2010 Personal Status Law.
66. www.mohamoon-ju.com/Print.aspx?op=0&ID=20318&Type=2&EG=1.
67. Articles 62-67 of the 1984 Libyan Personal Status Law.
68. Law No. 2008-20 of 4 March 2008, which amends Article 56 and Article 56a of the 1956 Personal Status Law.
69. Article 103 of the 1956 Tunisian Personal Status Law.
70. In October 2015, the National Human Rights Council of Morocco published a report on discrimination towards women in Morocco, in which it advocated equality between men and women with regard to inheritance (National Human Rights Council, 2015).
71. Law of 1998 that amended Article 20 of the code of registration fees and stamp duties.
72. See for instance Article 171 of the Tunisian 1956 Personal Status Law. The marriage age is 18 years for both men and women.

References

CEDAW (2015), "Sixth periodic report of States Parties due in 2016 (Jordan)", UN Committee on the Elimination of Discrimination Against Women (CEDAW), p. 50, http://tbinternet.ohchr.org/_layouts/treatybodyexternal/Download.aspx?symbolno=CEDAW%2fC%2fJOR%2f6&Lang=en.

CEDAW (2012), "Responses of Jordan to the list of issues to be taken up in connection with the consideration of its fifth periodic report", UN Committee on the Elimination of Discrimination Against Women (CEDAW), http://tbinternet.ohchr.org/_layouts/treatybodyexternal/Download.aspx?symbolno=CEDAW%2fC%2fJOR%2fQ%2f5%2fAdd.1&Lang=en.

CEDAW (1994), "General recommendation No. 21: Equality in marriage and family relations", UN Committee on the Elimination of Discrimination against Women (CEDAW), www.refworld.org/docid/48abd52c0.html.

Charmes, J. (2015), "Time use across the world: Findings of a world compilation of time use surveys", *2015 UNDP Human Development Report Background Paper*, UNDP Human Development Report Office, New York, http://hdr.undp.org/sites/default/files/charmes_hdr_2015_final.pdf.

Chiongson et al. (2011), "Role of law and justice in achieving gender equality", Background paper for *World Development Report 2012: Gender Equality and Development*, World Bank, Washington, DC, http://siteresources.worldbank.org/INTWDR2012/Resources/7778105-1299699968583/7786210-1322671773271/Chiongson-law-and-justice.pdf.

CNDH (2015), *L'Etat de la parité et de l'égalité au Maroc: Préserver et rendre effectifs les finalités et les objectifs constitutionnels*, Conseil National des Droits de l'Homme, Rabat, Morocco, www.cndh.ma/sites/default/files/cndh_-_r.e_web_-_parite_egalite_fr_-.pdf.

EBRD (2015), *Enhancing Women's Voice, Agency and Participation in the Economy*, European Bank for Reconstruction and Development, London, www.ebrd.com/gender/voice-agency.pdf.

El-Kholy, H. (2002), *Defiance and Compliance: Negotiating Gender in Low-Income Cairo*, Berghahn Books, New York/Oxford, p. 101, www.jstor.org/stable/j.ctt1btbw3k.

Esposito, J.L. and N. DeLong-Bas (2001), *Women in Muslim Family Law*, Syracuse University Press, Syracuse, NY.

Hassani-Nezhad, L. and A. Sjögren (2014), "Unilateral divorce for women and labor supply in the Middle East and North Africa: The effect of Khul' reform", *Feminist Economics*, Vol. 20/4, pp. 113-137, http://dx.doi.org/10.1080/13545701.2014.932421.

Moghadam, V. and F. Roudi-Fahimi (2005), "Reforming family laws to promote progress in the Middle East and North Africa" (policy brief), Population Reference Bureau, Washington, DC, available from www.prb.org/pdf06/ReformingFamilyLaws_MENA.pdf.

OECD (2016), "Tracking the money for women's economic empowerment: Still a drop in the ocean", OECD-DAC Network On Gender Equality (GENDERNET), OECD Publishing, Paris, www.oecd.org/dac/gender-development/tracking-money-for-womens-economic-empowerment.htm.

OECD (2010), *Progress in Public Management in the Middle East and North Africa: Case Studies on Policy Reform*, OECD Publishing, Paris, http://dx.doi.org/10.1787/9789264082076-en.

OECD, "Gender equality and women's rights in the post-2015 agenda: A foundation for sustainable development", https://www.oecd.org/dac/gender-development/POST-2015%20Gender.pdf.

Quarischi, A. and F.E. Vogel (2008), *The Islamic Marriage Contract: Cases Studies in Islamic Family Law*, Harvard Law School, Cambridge, Massachusetts.

UNDP (2006), *The Arab Human Development Report 2005: Towards the Rise of Women in the Arab World*, United Nations Development Programme Regional Bureau for Arab States, New York, http://hdr.undp.org/sites/default/files/rbas_ahdr2005_en.pdf.

UN (2015), "World Marriage Data 2015" (database), UN Department of Economic and Social Affairs, Population Division, United Nations, New York, www.un.org/en/development/desa/population/theme/marriage-unions/WMD2015.shtml.

Welchman, L. (2007), *Women and Muslim Family Laws in Arab States: A Comparative Overview of Textual Development and Advocacy*, Amsterdam University Press, Amsterdam, www.oapen.org/download?type=document&docid=340144.

World Bank (2016), *Women, Business and the Law*, The World Bank, Washington, DC, http://wbl.worldbank.org/~/media/WBG/WBL/Documents/Reports/2016/Women-Business-and-the-Law-2016.pdf.

World Bank (2013a), "Opening doors: Gender equality in the Middle East and North Africa", The World Bank, Washington, DC, https://openknowledge.worldbank.org/handle/10986/12552.

World Bank (2013b), "Country gender assessment: Economic participation, agency and access to justice in Jordan", World Bank, Washington, DC, http://documents.worldbank.org/curated/en/503361468038992583/Country-gender-assessment-economic-participation-agency-and-access-to-justice-in-Jordan.

World Bank (2011), *World Development Report 2012: Gender Equality and Development*, World Bank, Washington, DC, http://go.worldbank.org/6R2KGVEXP0.

World Bank (2009), *The Status and Progress of Women in the Middle East and North Africa*, World Bank, Washington, DC, http://siteresources.worldbank.org/INTMENA/Resources/MENA_Gender_Compendium-2009-1.pdf.

World Bank (2007), "Gender in the Middle East and North Africa", Gender Brief, World Bank, Washington, DC, http://go.worldbank.org/OIHU489AZ0.

World Bank (2004), *Gender and Development in the Middle East and North Africa: Women in the Public Sphere*, International Bank for Reconstruction and Development/ World Bank, Washington, DC, https://openknowledge.worldbank.org/handle/10986/15036.

World Bank (2001), *Engendering Development Through Gender Equality in Rights, Resources, and Voice,* Policy Research Report, World Bank, Washington, DC, http://documents.worldbank.org/curated/en/512911468327401785/Engendering-development-through-gender-equality-in-rights-resources-and-voice.

Chapter 4

Women's labour rights and entrepreneurship in selected MENA countries

This chapter examines women's labour rights in Algeria, Egypt, Jordan, Libya, Morocco and Tunisia. It considers labour law in terms of gender equality and non-discrimination, and reviews the impact of business law on women's entrepreneurship.

The chapter weighs women's right to equal terms in recruitment, promotion and pay against gender-based distinctions in employment benefits. It presents regulations that aim to protect women but may affect their capacity to work, and reviews entitlements to maternity and parental leave, the nursing of newborns at the workplace and childcare. It also examines the benefits and drawbacks for women of part-time and flex-time arrangements and early retirement.

The chapter assesses the business climate as it affects women, including enterprise registration, access to finance and networking. Violence and sexual harassment, as well as the quality of public transportation, are also considered in terms of how they affect women's ability to participate in the economy.

Introduction

MENA countries have taken a public stand in favour of gender equality through their international commitments and amendments to their constitutions. Women's educational attainment is rising in the region. Yet women's rates of participation in the labour force and entrepreneurship in MENA are well below those of men, and indeed are the lowest worldwide.

The labour codes of the countries under review provide for equal working rights and non-discrimination in recruitment and promotion, as well as equal wages for women and men. Yet, as this chapter will show, these norms are not always respected in practice. Provisions aimed at protecting women can limit their job opportunities. Measures in support of women like paid maternity leave, part-time employment or early retirement carry costs for private employers. Their effects can be counterproductive, reinforcing gender stereotypes and encouraging the recruitment and promotion of men.

This chapter also evaluates how the ability to establish, manage or develop a business differs according to gender in the six countries. Although laws affecting entrepreneurship are gender neutral, women experience gender-specific difficulties, particularly in access to finance and networks. Limited employment experience and earnings also create obstacles for women, as do sexual harassment and the poor quality of public transportation.

These impediments to women's participation in the economy may reflect a problem in the translation of international commitments on equality into domestic laws, and in the full implementation of those laws.

It should be noted that issues covered in this chapter relating to gender equality at the workplace remain a work in progress in many countries. Persistent challenges noted by the OECD include the stagnating labour force participation of women, gender wage gaps and entrenched discriminatory social norms and stereotypes.

Equal working rights but different benefits

States Parties to CEDAW and the ILO conventions commit to guaranteeing equal opportunities to all workers in the hiring process and during employment. Men and women are to be granted equal pay for equal work or for work of equal value.[1]

Equal opportunity to work and equal treatment in the public and private sectors are, in principle, guaranteed in the labour codes of the six countries. These codes, which build on countries' international commitments, regulate the relation between employers and employees for commencing, maintaining and terminating employment. All codes prohibit discrimination in relation to gender and pay.

It is noteworthy, however, that the labour codes of several countries do not cover certain categories of workers. In Egypt, for example, domestic workers and women in agriculture are excluded, whereas the labour codes of Jordan and Tunisia do not cover domestic, agricultural and irrigation workers and their families (OECD/CAWTAR 2014: 176). Considering the number of women involved in such activities, this is a major gap. The legislation results in an absence of protection for such workers.

The principle of non-discrimination

The labour codes of the six countries describe the rights and obligations of employees in neutral terms and prohibit discrimination.

- **Tunisia's** labour code prohibits all forms of discrimination between men and women.[2] The civil-service ordinance declares that it is illegal to differentiate between genders, "subject to the special provisions recommended by the nature of the duties".[3]
- In **Jordan**, the civil service regulation defines the principle of equal opportunity as prohibiting discrimination based on sex, race, religion or social status.[4] The labour code carries no explicit prohibition of direct or indirect discrimination against women in the private sector.[5]
- In **Libya**, the labour code guarantees equal job opportunities for men and women in the private and public sectors.[6]
- **Algeria**[7] and **Morocco**[8] expressly prohibit gender-related discrimination during recruitment and outlaw differences in workers' pay for equal qualifications and experience.
- In **Egypt**, the Labour Code explicitly prohibits wage discrimination based on sex, origin, language, religion or creed.[9]

Participants in focus groups in the countries under review noted that, despite the provisions for non-discrimination laid out in the labour codes, equal treatment and equal opportunities between men and women in the job market remain a challenge, particularly in the private sector. The participants stressed that women face significant gender-based inequalities, whether in relation to hiring, wages or career development (i.e. training and promotions), as reflected in the data presented in Chapter 1. In Jordan, despite non-discrimination provisions in the Civil Service Regulation, women encounter discrimination when seeking positions that are stereotypically male, such as technicians, mechanics, etc.[10]

As was also noted in Chapter 1, women rarely hold senior management positions in the public or private sector, and they are poorly represented on company boards of directors. In fact, none of the six countries has introduced regulations or adopted a voluntary quota policy with a view to developing women's corporate leadership and reducing the gender gap in the promotion of men and women.

Social norms set by family codes, discussed in the previous chapter, play an important role in the discrepancy between labour laws and practice in the MENA countries. For example, according to the focus groups, many employers view male employees as more committed to their jobs than their female counterparts. Participants reported that employers often preferred recruiting and investing in males, in particular when a job required travel; this may relate to the fact that men need no authorisation for their activities, in contrast to women. As mentioned in Chapter 2, in some countries women still need to obtain their husband's agreement to work and they bear responsibility for household chores. It was also noted that employers have strong expectations that women will stop working upon starting a family, as illustrated by the high workforce drop-out rate of women after the age of 29 (Figure 1.5, above). Moreover, in the event of economic redundancies, employers reportedly prefer dismissing a woman on the grounds that a man is the head of the household.

Compared to equally educated men, women tend to work in jobs requiring lower qualifications. Their career-development opportunities are affected, among other factors, by limitations on training and travelling abroad. As noted in Chapter 1, women are underrepresented in high-responsibility positions. This might be linked to the significant female drop-out rate from the labour force; many such positions become accessible only with considerable work experience. While the drop-out rate could be linked to women's homemaking responsibilities, one might also question whether and to what extent the difficulty of attaining senior positions may dissuade women from entering or staying in the labour market.

Box 4.1. **OECD framework on gender equality in leadership**

The OECD Council on Gender Equality in Education, Employment and Entrepreneurship (2013) recommends:[1]

1) increasing the representation of women in decision-making bodies by encouraging measures such as voluntary targets, disclosure requirements and private initiatives that enhance gender diversity on boards and in senior management of listed companies;

2) complementing such efforts with other measures to support effective board participation by women and expanding the pool of qualified candidates; and

3) continuing to monitor and analyse the costs and benefits of different approaches – including voluntary targets, disclosure requirements or boardroom quotas – to promote gender diversity in leadership positions in private companies.

These principles have been reiterated in the G20/OECD Principles of Corporate Governance (2015),[2] the revised OECD Guidelines on Corporate Governance of State-Owned Enterprises (2015)[3] and the OECD Council's Recommendation on Gender Equality in Public Life (2015).[4]

Notes:

1. www.oecd.org/gender/C-MIN(2013)5-ENG.pdf.
2. http://dx.doi.org/10.1787/9789264236882-en.
3. http://dx.doi.org/10.1787/9789264244160-en.
4. http://dx.doi.org/10.1787/9789264252820-en.

Women's high unemployment rate may be the result of employers' preference for recruiting and promoting men. However, focus group discussions also suggested that women's education may not be adequate for market needs, and that this might also affect their recruitment in the private sector.

Equivalent wages

Equal remuneration for equal work is a matter of rights and fairness. Equal valuation of men's and women's work and skills helps to increase women's autonomy. Raising women's earnings throughout their working life reduces their risk of falling into poverty, especially as they age.

The labour laws of Algeria,[11] Egypt,[12] Libya[13] and Morocco[14] promote equal pay by barring gender-related discrimination for equal work. The ILO committee of experts, however, considers that labour laws should provide not only for equal remuneration for men and women for equal or similar work, but should also address situations where men and women perform different jobs, using different skills and involving different working conditions, but which are nevertheless jobs or equal value.[15]

In spite of equal-pay provisions, and as noted in Chapter 1 and complemented by qualitative evidence from the focus groups, there continues to be a wage gap between women and men: women tend to receive an inferior wage for equal work, with the gaps particularly high in rural areas and in the private sector. Wage disparities in the public sector are far less pronounced.

As mentioned in the preceding chapter, social norms and family law provisions create a perception that women do not need to earn as much as men, and thus the view that wage disparities are justifiable. Participants in focus groups indicated that women are often assumed to bring in a secondary income, as opposed to men, who as heads of household are responsible for maintaining the family. This situation also exerts high pressure on men, as inside the households it is considered important for them to have a higher wage than the wife. Focus groups in Tunisia and Morocco indicated that the wage gap is considered an important feature for preserving the spousal relationship inside the household.

Different non-wage employment benefits

Employment benefits – in particular an efficient social security system that covers the costs of illness, hospitalisation and invalidity, and guarantees a pension or child benefits – may act as incentives for joining and remaining in formal employment.

Social protection is a constitutional right for men and women in Algeria,[16] Egypt,[17] Jordan,[18] Libya,[19] Morocco[20] and Tunisia.[21] Social security is financed by the employer, the employee and, to a lesser extent, the government, and in principle applies to men and women alike. The systems in place in the different countries generally allow married women to be covered through their husband's benefits when he is in formal employment. The problem arises for unmarried, divorced or widowed women working in informal employment.

- In **Algeria**, women who do not work are covered by their husband's or father's professional health insurance; women who work are covered in their own right.
- In **Egypt**,[22] social security is considered weak and its delivery costly. Many enterprises are not registered and avoid the obligations of formality. In other cases, employers try to circumvent paying social insurance for their employees, in particular women. The Egyptian Labour Market Panel Survey of 2006 suggested that only 10.51% of working females had a contractual agreement with their employers (Barsoum, 2010). The rate of female social security coverage does not surpass 20% in any age group, and it declines to as little as 3.7% for the ages 20-29 (Sieverding and Selwaness, 2012).
- In **Libya**, due to illiteracy and an absence of awareness of legal rights, a large proportion of female self-employed or private-sector workers do not understand the benefits and rights enshrined in the Social Security Act, reducing the real value of the laws for women.
- In **Jordan**, contributing to the social security system is mandatory.[23] Women who do not work are covered by their husband's or father's professional health insurance.[24] Access to inherited pensions becomes restricted if a woman remarries.[25] Male employees receive financial benefits to support their families, while women receive them only after proving they support their family.
- In **Tunisia**, women who do not work are covered by their parents until age 20 and by their husband upon marriage. If working, they will be covered and can ensure coverage for their husband if he is unemployed. Coverage is a problem for those

in informal employment, however, and measures put in place by the government (public health) are insufficient and are not accessible to all.

When available, child allowance payable to employees for the maintenance of their offspring can make a substantive contribution to income. Whereas no child benefit is paid in Egypt, a monthly allowance is available to married men employees in Algeria,[26] Jordan (only in the public sector),[27] Libya[28] and Morocco.[29] In these countries, women receive this benefit only if they are solely responsible for their family's financial support. Tunisia has introduced an exception: women working in a sector covered by the child-benefit regime can receive a very low allowance for children aged 2-36 months.[30]

Non-discriminatory labour legislation in the six countries does not prevent major gender gaps in recruitment, promotion and the termination of contracts, as shown in Chapter 1. Focus groups in the six countries provided observations on how gender differences build on social norms. Social security or child benefits seem to provide no strong incentives for women to engage in the formal sector: the welfare payments are generally available to married women through the formal employment of their husbands, and childcare is generally paid to the fathers. This is built on the assumption, written into the respective family codes, that men are responsible for the financial support of their families.

For the large number of women employees or entrepreneurs in sectors not covered by labour legislation or who work undeclared, the labour market is unregulated and unprotected. In light of the more favourable non-wage benefits or welfare payments granted to married men, it is worth examining to what extent joining the informal sector is a deliberate choice by women and their families.

Provisions aimed at protecting women

Laws seeking to regulate hazardous or strenuous work assume that women are more vulnerable than men and need to be protected. These laws may produce an adverse outcome, effectively restricting the employment available to women. Hence, these laws have been reconsidered at the international level.

ILO standards dealing with women's work have shifted from the original conception of the need to provide women with special protection against arduous working conditions, embedded in the 1958 Convention, towards the view that protection should be granted to all workers, irrespective of sex. Protective provisions are likely to further marginalise and sometimes even exclude women from the labour market and to perpetuate the belief that they are unable to decide for themselves. Such provisions also affect women's freedom to choose their profession. The ILO conventions dealing with night work[31] and work in mines[32] have thus been replaced by new treaties that apply to all workers, regardless of sex.

However, women's work and men's work are regulated differently in the six countries, which have enacted laws with a view to protecting women from exposure to dangers and difficulties.

Night work and sector restrictions

All six countries impose restrictions on women's work at night, especially in the private sector. The regulations vary by country: in Egypt, women are banned from working from 7 p.m. to 7 a.m.,[33] in Jordan[34] and Tunisia[35] from 10 p.m. to 6 a.m., in Algeria between 9 p.m. and 5 a.m.,[36] and in Libya from 8 p.m. to 7 a.m.[37] Morocco prohibits night work only for minors under 16,[38] but it imposes a minimum rest and recovery period for women between night shifts.[39]

The six countries have also adopted provisions regulating women's work in specific sectors or certain types of activities considered dangerous or morally harmful (Egypt[40] and Morocco[41]). This is the case, for example, for work in quarries or in mining (Morocco,[42] Tunisia,[43] Jordan[44] and Egypt[45]) or in establishments that salvage, transform or stock used metals (Tunisia[46]). In Libya, women may not undertake work that is not "familiar with woman's nature",[47] such as in oil fields. Under the Jordanian constitution, the Ministry of Labour enacts legislation establishing special conditions for the work of women and juveniles; the labour law also refers to the Ministry of Labour, which determines from what industries, jobs and times women are prohibited.[48]

Exceptions to these restrictions exist for certain jobs or sectors. There may be exceptions, for example, for women holding management positions (Tunisia,[49] Morocco,[50] Egypt[51]), or where the nature of the work and job description justify granting such an exemption (Algeria[52]). Exceptions can also be made for some work in hospitals, hotels, restaurants, cinemas or airports (Egypt,[53] Jordan[54]). Libya fixes the maximum number of hours per week that women can work (48), which prevents them from increasing their revenue through overtime pay.[55]

Although provisions regulating night work or women's involvement in certain sectors may be well intentioned, limitations designed to protect female workers are internationally considered out-of-date and discriminatory, as they reduce women's economic opportunities. By restricting women from working the same hours as men, these provisions distort their employment and income opportunities. By supporting the view that women are primarily caregivers rather than breadwinners, protective measures reinforce the gender divide. They work as a disincentive for employers to hire women, who are relegated to lower-paying sectors and activities.

Sector restrictions also have an impact on women's entrepreneurship. With women unable to gain work experience in certain high-paid sectors, like for instance mining in Egypt and Jordan, they cannot become entrepreneurs in those fields. That these sectors are often capital intensive creates another hurdle for women, who generally have less capital than men.

While all workers, men and women, should be protected from hazardous work, women should be able to decide for themselves on which job to take and which sector to choose. Gender-neutral laws would give women freedom of choice and increase their options and opportunities for entering the job market. Such laws would also improve recruitment for firms by potentially doubling the pool of candidates.

In order to enlarge the talent pool for recruitment, and with a view to introducing more flexibility in support of private-sector development, the governments of the six countries might consider abrogating laws regulating women's work at night and in certain sectors. It may be to the benefit of all, as experience in other countries has shown, to let women decide for themselves which duties they can assume or not (Box 4.2).

Box 4.2. **Countering gender stereotypes: a case study in Kazakhstan**

Gender stereotypes exist everywhere, but many countries are evolving. A project in the transportation sector in Kazakhstan, in partnership with the European Bank for Reconstruction and Development (EBRD), resulted in the hiring of the country's first women bus drivers.

Kazakhstan's labour code prohibits gender-based discrimination, and anyone who is subject to discrimination has the right to file proceedings in court (OECD, 2014b). However, the country's 2009 law on "Equal Rights and Equal Opportunities for Women and Men" applies only to public-sector employment (OECD, 2014b), and Article 186 of the labour code (2007) restricts women from performing work that is considered "heavy" or "harmful", and lists 299 restricted professions.

Occupational segregation in Kazakhstan mirrors gender norms and reinforces inequalities between women and men. Many of the jobs barred to women are in the construction and transport sectors, where pay is typically higher (ADB, 2013). Conversely, women represent more than 70% of employees in low-paying sectors such as education and health care. Furthermore, the glass ceiling continues to block women from advancing in their careers, as shown by the low number of women in leadership and managerial positions (ADB, 2013).

To break down occupational segregation and address discrimination against women in employment, the EBRD has worked on a promising project in Kazakhstan in the male-dominated urban transport sector. From 2013 to 2015, the EBRD worked with Almaty's public transport operator, Almatyelectrotrans (AET), to promote equal opportunities for women and men in the urban transport sector and increase the number of women bus drivers. Women are typically discouraged from pursuing a career in the sector, due in part to discriminatory attitudes on appropriate employment for women, but also to legal barriers such as discriminatory licensing requirements (EBRD, 2015).

AET adopted gender-responsive strategies that led to the recruitment in 2015 of the first female bus driver. These include: recruitment policies that actively encourage women to apply, a new monitoring system for collecting sex-disaggregated workforce data and a company commitment to equal opportunities. Positive outcomes include an increase in the proportion of women in management, from 19% in 2014 to 28% in 2015; women hired in technical operations, which were previously all-male positions; and the recruitment of a second woman bus driver in 2015, which established a positive role model and contributes to changing attitudes. AET managers and staff also reported improved awareness of equal opportunity within the organisation (EBRD, 2015).

Source: ADB (2013), Kazakhstan Country Gender Assessment, OECD (2015), SIGI Regional Report: Europe and Central Asia, www.adb.org/sites/default/files/institutional-document/34051/files/kazakhstan-country-gender-assessment.pdf (accessed 15 October 2015).

Maternity benefits

Maternity benefits include paid leave before and after childbirth, security to return to one's job after maternity leave and the possibility to nurse one's child upon resumption of work. These provisions aim to ensure a good work-life balance for working mothers upon the arrival of their children.

The 2000 ILO Maternity Protection Convention declares it unlawful for an employer to terminate the employment of a woman during her pregnancy (Article 8). In line with this, women are protected against termination of their employment contract during pregnancy and maternity leave in Morocco and Tunisia,[56] Egypt[57] and Jordan.[58] (there is no provision in the civil service regulation for public sector employees). In Algeria, pregnant women are not expressly protected against termination of their work contract by a specific provision, but like other employees women are protected against unfair dismissal. In Libya, a woman's work may not be terminated during pregnancy or maternity leave except when there are "justifiable reasons that are not related to pregnancy and maternity and birth complications or breast feeding."

Maternity and paternity leave

Under the revised 2000[59] ILO Maternity Protection Convention, maternity leave should be no less than 14 weeks and should include a period of at least 6 weeks after childbirth (Article 4).[60] Article 6 states that the cash benefits "shall be at a level which ensures that the woman can maintain herself and her child in proper conditions of health and with a suitable standard of living." Where provided through compulsory social insurance and based on previous earnings, the amount of such benefits shall not be less than two-thirds of the woman's previous earnings. The ILO notes that reducing the direct costs of maternity leave for the employer will "help to prevent discrimination and protect the situation of women workers in the labour market" (ILO, 2013: 41). There is now a view that rights should also be considered for fathers. The importance of providing employment-protected paid maternity and paternity leave to working mothers and fathers is underlined by the 2013 OECD Gender Recommendations.

Of the six countries under review, only Morocco has ratified the ILO 2000 Maternity Protection Convention. Maternity leave is granted in all six countries, but the duration varies across countries and between the public and the private sector, with payments covered by different stakeholders (Table 4.1). Short paternity leave is possible in Algeria, Libya, Morocco and Tunisia.

Table 4.1. **Conditions of maternity leave**

Country	Length of leave	Coverage amount (%)	Financed by
Algeria	14 weeks	100	Social security
Egypt	90 days	100	Mixed (75% social insurance, 25% employer)
Jordan	90 days (public) 70 days (private)	100	Social security
Libya	14 weeks	50	Employer
Morocco	14 weeks	100	Social security
Tunisia	30 days (private) 60 days (public)	67 (private sector) 100 (public sector)	Social security

Source: Adapted from the World Bank based on data from MENA countries.

In Algeria, Libya and Morocco, women are granted 14 weeks of maternity leave. In Algeria and Morocco, the costs are covered by the government and/or the social security system, while in Libya employers must pay the leave. Payment by the employer is also the rule in Egypt, where female employees can benefit from up to two 90-day maternity leaves on full pay during their working life, provided they have worked for the employer for at least 10 months.[61] In Jordan, the leave is about 13 weeks in the public sector and 10 weeks in the private sector, where employers and male and female employees have contributed since 2010 to a Maternity Fund managed by the Social Security Corporation. In Tunisia, maternity leave is 30 days in the private sector.[62] Collective labour agreements in specific sectors call for payment of the leave by the employer (e.g. banks, insurance), but in general the National Social Security Fund ensures a daily allowance to compensate for a woman's suspended salary, provided she has been employed for at least 80 days.[63] In Tunisia's public sector, the maternity leave of 60 days is paid in full.[64]

Financial structures that put the burden of maternity leave on the private employer may need to be revised, as they invite discrimination against women, in particular of child-bearing age.

Paternity leave allows new fathers to take a short period of leave in order to bond with the new-born and help the mother take care of the child. The purpose is also to help dissociate the costs of child-rearing from women and to recognise fathers' family responsibilities. Paternity leave reflects evolving views of fatherhood and parenting roles, with greater involvement of fathers around childbirth and in the domestic sphere. In Algeria,[65] Morocco[66] and Libya, the father is allowed to take three days of paternity leave. The costs are covered by the employer in Algeria and by social security in Morocco. In Tunisia, a two-day leave is granted, the cost of which is covered by social security.[67] No paternity leave is available in Egypt, Jordan or Libya.

Box 4.3. **Gender-sensitive employment practices in the public sector in MENA**

The public sector is the most prominent employer of women in the MENA region, as it is in many OECD countries. However, a 2014 OECD study showed that the region's women are less represented in senior positions and tend to earn lower salaries than men in the public sector. Potential sources of inequality include pay and job classification, recruitment, promotion and evaluation, and access to professional development, even when legal texts constitute a strong framework for gender equality. Nonetheless, the region is making important progress in establishing measures to support combined responsibilities for family and work.

Gender-responsive human resources strategy in the public sector

Egypt and Morocco can be cited as examples of proactive approaches to strengthening gender balance in the MENA public sector. The two countries report conducting gender-balance assessments of the government workforce. Both have taken steps to increase women's representation in sectors where they are traditionally less present, such as integrating gender-diversity targets into performance agreements for top management (Morocco) and giving preference to equally qualified women in the civil-service selection process (Egypt).

On the supply side, there are only a few leadership development programmes in the region. One example of good practice exists in Morocco's initiatives to strengthen gender balance in public employment and reduce the gender pay gap. The country's Ministry of Public Sector Modernisation (MMSP) published a handbook as a first step towards a broader reform of pay and classification. It reviews whether current requirements or job descriptions disadvantage women or discourage them from applying so that these sources of discrimination can be corrected. Concerning professional development, the MMSP conducted a study to identify female civil servants' needs in leadership development and management capacity building, and completed a study on reconciling family and professional life as the basis for developing gender-responsive training programmes.

Box 4.3. **Gender-sensitive employment practices in the public sector in MENA** *(continued)*

Work-life balance measures for civil service employees

Not unlike in OECD countries, the public sector in the MENA region is seen as offering much greater compatibility between family and professional duties than the private sector. For example, specific measures for women who are breastfeeding, which exist in most of the MENA countries, include additional breaks and specified nursing areas for women (Bahrain, Egypt, Jordan, Kuwait, Morocco, the Palestinian Authority, Tunisia and Yemen). Leaves to care for family members who are ill, particularly children, are also often provided for women (Bahrain, Egypt, Jordan, Kuwait and Morocco). Pregnant women benefit from additional measures to facilitate work-life balance (Bahrain, Egypt, Jordan, Kuwait and Yemen). This may include provisions for specific physical changes in the work environment to accommodate pregnancy and restrictions on strenuous labour. In some cases, women also receive additional time off to care for elderly family members (Bahrain, Egypt, Jordan and Tunisia). Flexible work-time options can also improve the gender balance in the work place. While some countries report using flexible working hours in the public sector (Bahrain, Egypt and Yemen) and a compressed working week (Bahrain), the use of these measures is very rare across the region.

Nevertheless, work-life balance measures across the region tend to support the traditional responsibilities of women in the household, particularly in relation to their reproductive and caretaker roles (pregnancy, breastfeeding, leave to care for a sick family member), with less emphasis on other measures that could improve work-life balance (telework, compressed work weeks and flexible working hours).

Source: OECD (2015d), *Women in Public Life: Gender, Law and Policy in the Middle East and North Africa.*

Nursing of children

A mother's decision to return to work also depends on the possibility of nursing her child. Accordingly, the 2000 ILO Maternity Protection Convention (Article 10) states that a woman shall be provided the right to one or more daily breaks or a daily reduction of work time in order to breastfeed her child. It says that these breaks or the reduction of daily hours of work shall be counted as working time and remunerated accordingly. But the convention leaves it to national laws to determine the number and duration of nursing breaks.[68]

The six countries grant nursing employees two paid half-hour breaks per day to breastfeed during working hours. This applies for a period of one year in Morocco,[69] Jordan[70] and Tunisia,[71] 18 months in Libya[72] and two years in Egypt.[73] In Algeria, public-sector employees benefit from two hours of rest per day during the first six months after a birth and one hour per day for the six months thereafter.[74]

While meant to protect women and their children, maternity benefits also seek to enhance women's productivity and ensure their involvement in economic life. Maternity leave represents a significant expense, however, in particular if funded solely by the private-sector employer. Maternity and breast-feeding expenses can deter the hiring of women of reproductive age, leading entrepreneurs to favour men during the recruitment process or to pay women less. This was underscored in focus group discussions, where participants also mentioned that certain private-sector employers make their female employees sign a blank letter of resignation upon recruitment for later use, for instance in order to force a woman to leave when pregnant. It was mentioned that only large enterprises, including multinationals operating in the countries, are of sufficient scale to absorb the costs generated by their employees' maternity leave. Obviously, maternity benefits do not apply to informal female employees.

Governments may consider evaluating whether the differences pertaining to public- and private-sector maternity leave are supportive of an effective labour market. They may consider introducing the same leave periods for public- and private-sector employees, in line with international standards. They should also evaluate and put into place systems limiting employers' direct or indirect costs associated with maternity leave and nurturing. Providing government assistance would be one option to reduce employers' costs and thus to further the recruitment of women.

Box 4.4. **Supporting early education services for children in Indonesia**

Since the early 2000s, Indonesia has put considerable effort into the expansion of programmes and financing mechanisms to stimulate access to pre-primary education for children from the poorest and most vulnerable segments in society. Beginning in 2002, the Ministry of National Education (MONE) has provided subsidies to support the provision of early childhood education services through private institutions and non-profit organisations. The government approved block grants for local level initiatives to finance the costs of materials and teacher training for formal programmes, as well as offer subsidies for non-formal programmes. The communities were then given the autonomy to effectively dispurse the funds based on need.

In 2006, a new set of block grants were introduced to support community-based, non-formal services. The grant programme partnered with local governments by matching funds and allocating resources. It targeted approximately 738 000 children, aged 0-6, residing in 3 000 villages within 50 districts that were characterised with a high prevalence of poverty and low enrolment rates in early childcare institutions.

The unique feature of the block grant programmes is that they are structured so local governments and the community are strategically involved in the decision making process. Local level management of programme initiatives, working within the guidelines of central institutions, has been particularly effective in increasing the enrolment of children from disadvantaged backgrounds and those residing in remote areas. Through the inclusion of local collaboration, the block grant programmes succeeded in addressing several challenges that used to constraint access to early childhood education in the country, such as: limited facilities, unequal distribution of services between rural and urban areas, poor staffing, and lack of financial capacity for families to pay school tuition fees.

Notable progress has been made towards expanding access to institutional childcare. Although rigorous assessments of the direct effects of block grant programmes are not yet available, descriptive statistics indicate that their contribution to the overall improvement in access to early childhood facilities may be significant. Net enrolment rates have almost doubled in less than a decade, increasing from 22% in 2005 to 41% in 2014, and have been associated with positive effects on the well-being of children in the programme. The mortality rate for children under 5 years of age has declined from 41/1 000 births in 2005 to 28.2/1 000 births in 2014, while the prevalence of stunting in children in the same age range has fallen from 40% in 2007 to 36% in 2013.

Source: UNESCO Institute for Statistics.

Parental benefits and childcare

Parental leave is paid or unpaid time off to care for a newborn after maternity leave. It can in principle be granted to either parent. Like childcare, it is meant to facilitate reconciliation of work and family responsibilities without loss of employment. Parental leave, while not included in any of the ILO conventions, is referenced in recommendations that accompany them. These do not, however, specify the duration of leave, payment or other aspects such as the conditions of the leave or the distribution of the leave between parents.

In the six countries under review, parental leave for the mother has been introduced in Egypt, Jordan, Morocco and Tunisia, mostly as an unpaid benefit in the private sector when available:

- In **Egypt**, female employees in the public sector are entitled to take up to three parental leaves of up to two years without pay,[75] whereas only employees of private companies employing more than 50 people are allowed a maximum of two years' leave without pay.[76]
- In **Jordan**, mothers can take parental leave without pay for up to two years in the public sector[77] but only one year in the private sector.[78]
- In **Morocco**, women can request unpaid leave for one year with a guarantee that their job will be available upon their return.[79]
- In **Tunisia**, post-natal leave is available in the public sector for the mother upon request for a maximum of four months at half pay.[80] No parental leave is available in the private sector.

Participants in focus groups indicated that private sector employers are frequently hostile to parental leave, and that mothers taking such leave rarely find themselves in an equivalent job when returning to work.

As studies have highlighted (OECD, 2012: 203) and as underlined during focus group discussions, policies aiming to support parental leave for both parents may inadvertently reinforce the more traditional role of women as caregivers, since it is primarily mothers who make use of parental leave entitlements. In OECD countries, one reason for fathers' low take-up rate is that they frequently earn more than their spouses and the loss to the household income is thus higher if they take the leave. This factor could apply even more strongly in the six countries in light of the fact that non-wage employment benefits are primarily made available to men.

Box 4.5. **Father-specific parental leave and the gender pay gap**

A number of studies show the link between the gender pay gap and the division of labour in the home. A study in the United States found that companies offer different remuneration to women and men based on expectations of their share of work in the household (Albanesi and Olivetti, 2006). Another study of 15 developed countries found that where men do a greater share of housework, the gender pay gap is lower (Chichilnisky and Frederiksen, 2008). In a number of countries a "motherhood penalty" has been identified whereby the gender pay gap is greater for women with children than those without (Correll, Benard and Paik, 2007). Encouraging greater sharing of care responsibilities, for example through paid paternity leave or "fathers-only" paid parental leave, is therefore important (OECD, 2016b). A review of legislation in 126 countries and territories indicates that 42 have laws in place to guarantee paid paternity leave (World Bank, 2010).

Box 4.5. **Father-specific parental leave and the gender pay gap** *(continued)*

The government of Sweden has had a policy of paid parental leave since 1974, with women and men equally entitled to take time off. However, in practice women took the majority of the allocated leave, so the policy was amended in 1995 and 2002 to encourage greater take-up among fathers through the introduction of "daddy months" which are non-transferable to the mother. A study has found that for every month of leave a father takes, a mother's earnings increase by an average of 6.7%, counteracting the "motherhood penalty" (Johansson, 2010). Because of policies like this, as well as the provision of high-quality childcare, the gender pay gap in Sweden is 13%, significantly lower than other countries in Europe such as Hungary (18%) and Spain (23%) (Glenn, Melis and Withers, 2009).

Following the success of the Swedish daddy months, a growing number of OECD countries have now introduced paid parental leave to be used only by the father. By and large, these periods of fathers-only leave have been successful. For example, in Iceland, the introduction in 2001 of a three-month fathers-only quota saw the share of paid leave days taken by fathers increase from just under 3% in 2000 to almost 32% in 2004 (OECD, 2016c). Similarly, in Germany, the proportion of children with a father who used at least some parental leave increased dramatically – from 8.8% for children born in 2007 to 32% for children born in 2013 – following the introduction in 2007 of a two-month "bonus period" available when both parents take at least two months of leave (Reich, 2010). Reserving periods of leave for the father does not, of course, guarantee that fathers will take leave: Korea, for example, now reserves one year of paid parental leave just for the father, but men still make up only around 5% of parental-leave users (Destatis, 2015). Still, the success of fathers-only entitlements in many OECD countries suggests they are one of the most important tools available to policymakers looking to promote fathers' leave.

Sources:

Albanesi, S. and C. Olivetti (2006), "Home Production, Market Production and the Gender Wage Gap: Incentives and Expectations".

Chichilnisky, G. and E. Hermann Frederiksen (2008), "An equilibrium analysis of the gender wage gap".

Correll, S., S. Benard, and I. Paik (2007), "Getting a Job: Is there a Motherhood Penalty?".

Destatis (2015), *Statistik zum Elterngeld Beendete Leistungsbezüge für im Jahr 2013 geborene Kinder: Januar 2013 bis März 2015*, https://www.destatis.de/DE/Publikationen/Thematisch/Soziales/Elterngeld/ElterngeldGeburtenJ_5229201139004.pdf?__blob=publicationFile.

Glenn, S., S. Melis and L. Withers (2009), "Gender (in)equality in the labour market: An overview of global trends and developments".

Johansson, E. (2010), "The effect of own and spousal parental leave on earnings".

OECD (2016b), *Dare to Share: Germany's Experience Promoting Equal Partnership in Families*, http://dx.doi.org/10.1787/9789264259157-en.

OECD (2016c), *OECD Family Database*.

Reich, N. (2010), "Who cares? Determinants of the fathers' use of parental leave in Germany", www.hwwi.org/fileadmin/hwwi/Publikationen/Research/Paper/Wirtschaftliche_Trends_und_HH/HWWI_Research_Paper_1-31.pdf.

World Bank (2010), "Women, Business and the Law: Measuring Legal Gender Parity for Entrepreneurs and Workers in 128 Economies".

UN Women (2011), *Progress of the World's Women: In Pursuit of Justice*.

The ease and affordability of care for young children and free public education can be decisive in a woman's choice to resume a professional activity outside the home, whereas a lack of childcare options can lead to career interruptions and discontinuous employment.

CEDAW's Article 11(2)(c) provides that States Parties shall take appropriate measures "to encourage the provision of the necessary supporting social services to enable parents to combine family obligations with work responsibilities and participation in public life, in particular through promoting the establishment and development of a network of childcare facilities." The ILO 1981 Convention concerning Equal Opportunities and Equal Treatment for Men and Women Workers: Workers with Family Responsibilities (Article. 5b) states: "All measures compatible with national conditions and possibilities shall further be taken… to develop or promote community services, public or private, such as childcare and family services and facilities."

The labour codes in Jordan,[81] Morocco,[82] Egypt[83] and Libya[84] require private-sector employers to provide childcare facilities on site when they employ more than a specific number of women. In Jordan, for example, a private-sector employer with 20 or more married women employees must provide childcare facilities if the women collectively have at least ten children under the age of four. Jordan's 2013 Civil Service Code does not require the provision of such facilities for children, but an internal circular issued in 2015 requests public entities' compliance with this labour provision. The minimum number of women employees for mandatory provision of childcare facilities is 50 in Morocco and Libya and 100 in Egypt. In Algeria and Tunisia, neither the private nor the public sector is required to provide nurseries.

In practice, the obligation of private-sector employers to provide parental leave and childcare for female employees exerts a negative influence on women's recruitment and the payment of salaries equal to men's. Focus group participants mentioned that some employers avoid reaching the threshold number of women employees that require them to provide childcare facilities; others do not employ married women. All of this eventually has a high cost for society and negatively affects both company growth and society.

Current child-care provisions also limit women entrepreneurs' options for care of their children while operating their business.

In the absence of adequate, secure, sufficient and affordable childcare facilities, women tend to take a temporary break from work or even abandon their careers altogether. This can create a vicious circle for gender inequality, for if women reduce their participation in employment when they have children, employers may choose to invest less in their female employees.

On the other hand, it could be argued that mother-specific childcare policies, which are meant to encourage and support the participation of mothers in the labour market, inadvertently reinforce the more traditional role of women as caregivers and in that sense perpetuate gender inequality.

To support parents in their decisions about family and work, governments should put into place state-supported childcare facilities. For parents, this would diminish the costs and career implications of having a child. It would also limit the financial obligations of private employers, allowing them to consider the recruitment of young women in a more positive manner. Women would have the comfort of resuming work while care for young children is granted, and the costs associated with maternity leave and childcare would not have to be supported solely by private employers.

Allowing men and women to benefit from government-backed childcare options as well as parental leave may work in support of a more diversified labour market and stronger gender equality. It may also help women engage in entrepreneurship, allowing them time to establish and develop their business.

Box 4.6. **Childcare services, female employment and child outcomes in OECD countries**

Supplying childcare services fosters female employment

The development of childcare services plays a key role in enabling parents, especially mothers, to maintain their participation in the labour market after childbirth. Thévenon (2013; 2016) suggests that an increase in the coverage of childcare services for children under age 3 led to a significant increase in the employment rate of women aged 25-54 from the early 1990s to 2008. This represents about one-fourth of the total increase in female employment over the period. The effect of childcare on female labour supply varies across countries and is strongest in countries with robust overall support for working parents, as in the Nordic countries, including leave, employment protection and tax incentives to work.

Early childhood education and care (ECEC) services do not benefit all population groups to the same extent, however. Children of wealthier families and whose mothers have a tertiary diploma are most likely to be enrolled in formal childcare services (OECD, 2016d), and the availability of childcare facilities seems to have a greater influence on the likelihood of returning to work for mothers with a tertiary degree than for mothers with a lower level of educational attainment (Del Boca et al., 2009; Cipollone, 2014).

Does formal childcare enhance child outcomes?

The OECD (2011; 2009) provides ample evidence of the positive effects on children's outcomes of investing early in ECEC services. Investing in early childhood services increases the efficiency of later investment ("skills beget skills"), and helps save money that is otherwise required later to repair the long-term consequences of underinvestment in human capital (Heckman and Masterov, 2007; Duncan and Magnussen, 2013).

Formal childcare participation is found to have positive effects on the cognitive development of children as well as on their behavioural development and school achievement (Ruhm and Waldfogel, 2011). The effects are stronger for disadvantaged children, while they are sometimes ambiguous for children of wealthy families and/or with highly educated parents due to their access to better alternative childcare solutions compared with low-quality centre-based services (van Huizen and Plantenga, 2015).

The quality of services and intensity of care are two parameters that matter. Long hours in care is associated with more behavioural problems because children are tired and exposed to stressful situations, and sometimes with poorer developmental outcomes, but these effects are small and vary with child characteristics (Belsky et al., 2007; Bradley and Vandell, 2007; Stein et al., 2013). At the same time, a high-quality centre-based care environment is found to foster children's cognitive development and to increase levels of pre-academic skills and language at four years of age (NICHD, 2001; 2003). There is also evidence that the earlier children start pre-school, the more positive the outcomes (for England, Sylva et al., 2011; for France, Fougère et al., 2014).

There is some evidence of positive long-term effects of attending pre-school programmes. Data from the OECD's Programme for International Student Assessment (PISA) show that 15-year-old students who attended pre-primary education for at least a year are likely to have higher mathematics scores than those who did not, the gap being equivalent to almost one year of formal schooling after accounting for students' socio-economic status (OECD, 2013). The participation in ECEC programmes can also be associated with increased employment, lower teenage pregnancy rates, higher socio-economic status, decreased criminal behaviour and reduced welfare dependency (Havnes and Mogstad, 2011; van Huizen and Plantenga, 2015).

Box 4.6. **Childcare services, female employment and child outcomes in OECD countries** *(continued)*

Investing in childcare programmes also delivers positive effects for health. Ludwig and Miller (2007) found that Head Start programmes in the United States have been responsible for a large drop in mortality of children aged five to nine, while Anderson et al. (2010) estimate that the same programmes have diminished the risk of smoking in young adulthood by 25% compared with other pre-school programmes.

Sources:

Anderson, K.H., J.E. Foster and D.E. Frisvold (2010), "Investing in health: The long-term impact of Head Start on smoking".

Belsky, J. et al. (2007), "Are there long-term effects of early childcare?", http://onlinelibrary.wiley.com/doi/10.1111/j.1467-8624.2007.01021.x/pdf.

Bradley, R.H. and D.L. Vandell (2007), "Child care and the well-being of children".

Cipollone A., E. Patacchini and G. Vallanti (2014), "Female labour market participation in Europe: Novel evidence on trends and shaping factors".

Del Boca D., S. Pasqua and Ch. Pronzato (2009), "Motherhood and market work decisions in institutional context: A European perspective".

Duncan, G. J. and K. Magnuson. (2013), "Investing in preschool programs".

Fougère D., O. Filatriau and M. To (2014), "Will sooner be better?: The impact of early preschool enrollment on cognitive and noncognitive achievement of children".

Havnes T., and M. Mogstad (2011), "No child left behind: Subsidized child care and children's long-run outcomes".

Heckman, J. and D. Masterov (2007), "The productivity argument for investing in young children".

Heckman J. et al. (2010), "A new cost-benefit and rate of return analysis for the Perry Preschool Program: A summary".

Ludwig, J. and D. Miller (2007), "Does Head Start improve children's life chances? Evidence from a regression discontinuity design".

National Institute for Child Health and Human Development Early Child Care Network (NICHD) (2003), "Does amount of time in child care predict socio-emotional adjustment during the transition to kindergarten?".

National Institute for Child Health and Human Development Early Child Care Network (NICHD) (2001), "Nonmaternal care and family factors in early development: An overview of the NICHD study of early child care".

OECD (2016d), "Who uses childcare? Inequalities in the use of formal early childhood education and care (ECEC) among very young children", www.oecd.org/els/family/database.htm.

OECD (2013), *PISA 2012 Results: Excellence Through Equity: Giving Every Student the Chance to Succeed*, http://dx.doi.org/10.1787/9789264201132-en.

OECD (2011), *Doing Better for Families*, http://dx.doi.org/10.1787/9789264098732-en.

OECD (2009), *Doing Better for Children*, http://dx.doi.org/10.1787/empl_outlook-2010-en.

Ruhm, C. and J. Waldfogel (2011), "Long-term effects of early childhood care and education".

Stein A. et al. (2013), "The influence of different forms of early childcare on children's emotional and behavioural development at school entry".

Sylva, K., I. Siraj-Blatchford and B. Taggart (2011).

Thévenon O. (2016), "Do 'institutional complementarities' foster female labour force participation?".

Thévenon, O. (2013), "Drivers of female labour force participation in the OECD", http://dx.doi.org/10.1787/5k46cvrgnms6-en.

van Huizen, Th., and J. Plantenga (2015), "Universal child care and children's outcomes: A meta-analysis of evidence from natural experiments".

Flexible time arrangements

The 1981 ILO Convention concerning Equal Opportunities and Equal Treatment for Men and Women Workers encourages States Parties to provide special measures for men and women with family responsibilities: "Each Member shall make it an aim of national policy to enable persons with family responsibilities who are engaged or wish to engage in employment to exercise their right to do so without being subject to discrimination and, to the extent possible, without conflict between their employment and family responsibilities."

By allowing the combination of a profession with family duties, flexibility in working hours, teleworking or part-time employment can give employees more control over their working time and decrease stress and health problems. Flexible time arrangements allow employees to organise their working hours in co-ordination with those of other employees and to fix the beginning or the end of the day around core hours of presence. Teleworking, i.e. working from home, eliminates the need to commute one or several days a week, as employees can engage with colleagues, customers or central offices through modern technologies. Part-time work involves fewer working hours than a full-time job, but it often implies lower hourly earnings, fewer promotion opportunities, less trainings, and reduced access to employment insurance, pension entitlements or unemployment benefits. To prevent discrimination, international labour standards require that the transfer from full-time to part-time work be voluntary and that part-time workers receive protection, basic wages and social security as well as employment conditions equivalent to those accorded to comparable full-time workers.[85]

Box 4.7. **Easing restrictions on part time work as a possible solution to decreasing informality for women**

In many countries, labour laws designed to protect workers may inadvertently harm economic opportunities for women and encourage informality. Existing regulations that discourage part-time work, either by means of implicit fiscal disincentives (e.g. high mandated minimum social security contributions) or by placing excessive restrictions on the use of part-time contracts, are instances where the unintended consequences of legislation can have a determental impact on women's economic opportunities. Argentina, seeking to find a solution to such situations, found a remedy by removing a ban on part-time work. The result was a significant shift from informal work to formal part-time employment among women (Bosch and Maloney, 2010; World Bank, 2012a). The desirability of such policies will depend on the specific circumstances of each country and on a careful assessment of the potential drawbacks that removing existing regulations might entail (e.g. the potential negative effects of part-time work on women's career progression).

Source: Strengthening Women's Entrepreneurship in Asean, OECD (forthcoming).

The labour codes of Algeria, Egypt, Libya and Tunisia provide for part-time work, but the provisions do not always apply to men and are mostly for public-sector employees. Teleworking is allowed only in Algeria. None of the six countries references flexible time.

- In **Algeria**, an employee may ask to work part time for personal convenience, subject to the employer's agreement.[86] The pay of part-time workers must be proportional to that of employees of the same employer who are equally qualified and occupy equivalent posts on a full-time basis, unless more favourable terms are agreed upon.[87] Teleworking is also possible.[88]

- In **Egypt**, a public-sector female employee may request half-time work for half pay.[89]
- In **Libya**, women may request to work part-time in all administrative, service and productive jobs.[90] Working hours shall not exceed 4 hours per day and 24 hours a week. The employer pays 60% of the salary, and social security 40%.
- In **Tunisia**, male and female employees in the private sector may ask for part-time work in order to look after a child below the age of six or a disabled or sick member of the family.[91] In the public sector, women may work part-time and receive up to two-thirds of their salary.

Employers in the six countries do not favour flexible-time arrangements, which have not been introduced in a systematic manner in the public or private sector.

According to the focus groups, part-time arrangements tend to reinforce gender stereotypes, and this in turn incites employers to favour male recruitment and promotions. Participants also noted that employers distrusted telework, fearing that employees who worked from home would not do their share. Women entrepreneurs in high-tech industries, though, reported very positive experiences of working from home and connecting virtually with worldwide employees. They noted that teleworking and flex-time contributed to high productivity in their businesses, and suggested that high-technology and high-growth companies can operate perfectly and achieve impressive results with dedicated employers working in different time zones through new technologies. Companies operating in such industries and in such a manner occasionally choose to register in countries outside MENA while maintaining an operating base within the region.

Governments should assess the possibility of introducing provisions granting more flexible working conditions. They may do so in consultation with business associations and trade unions in order to ensure that these arrangements provide for effective flexibility and do not introduce rigidity. States should also consider encouraging the introduction of measuring productivity rather than time spent at work. Flexible work arrangements may be particularly relevant in light of women's considerations regarding transportation (see discussion below). A careful balance should be sought, however, to avoid confining women who work on a flexible basis to limited access to work, careers or presence in the public sphere, as networking in person and interaction with other employees and managers are also important.

Retirement age and taxation

Gender-based regulations on retirement and income taxes may incentivise, or limit, the respective entry of women and men into the labour market.

Retirement entitlements vary from country to country, as do pension outcomes for men and women. Gender differences in labour-market experiences affect pension financing. The length of working periods leading up to retirement may also influence recruitment decisions.

Under ILO international standards, the retirement age should not exceed 65.[92] Benefits should be secured to persons who have completed 30 years of contribution or employment,[93] and a reduced benefit shall be secured to persons who have completed at least 15 years of contributions.

In the six countries under review, gender plays a significant role in determining retirement benefits, eligible beneficiaries and the circumstances under which benefits are granted in the case of the death of a spouse. Usually, retirement age is lower for women than for men (Table 4.2).

Table 4.2. **Retirement age in the six countries**

	Men	Women	Early retirement
Algeria	60	55[1]	• Women from the age of 45 if they have worked for at least 15 years and contributed to social security for at least 7-1/2 of those years
Egypt	60	60[2]	• For both men and women in the public and private sectors after at least 20 years of contribution
Jordan	60	55 in the private sector[3] 60 in the public sector[4]	
Libya	65	60	
Morocco	60	60	• Women from the age of 55 in the private sector if they have worked at least 3 240 days[5] • after 15 years of service in the public sector (as opposed to 21 years for men)[6]
Tunisia	60	60	• In the public sector, upon request for mothers of three children or a child with a severe handicap;[7] • in the private sector, mothers of three can request to retire at 50 if they have contributed at least 180 months, i.e. 15 years, of work

Notes:

1. Article 6 of the 1983 Law on Social Insurance.
2. Article 18 para. 1 of the 1975 Law Promulgating the Social Insurance Law. Retirement age for men and women in private and public sectors is 60 years of age, with 120 months of contribution (10 years).
3. Article 63(a) of the Social Security Law.
4. Article 12 of the Civil Service Retirement Law.
5. Article 13 of the 1980 Social Security Law and Article 43 of the 2010 Labour Relations Law.
6. Article 526 of the 2003 Labour Law
7. Article 24 of the 1985 Law on Civil Pension and military retirement and survivors in the public sector, as amended in 1988.

It is noteworthy that spouses may obtain pension entitlements from the deceased. In particular, widows are entitled to the pension of the deceased husband. In Jordan, women may also be entitled to portions from their deceased parents. This does not, however, compensate for the desirability for women of building up their own pension rights.

Early retirement is often considered to be a benefit in the six countries, though such a measure can have adverse financial effects for women and work against their employment. Retiring early not only limits the ability to build up pension entitlements (OECD, 2012), but may exacerbate women's poverty in old age, since women have a higher life expectancy but lower savings than men. Women who have taken career breaks to rear their children will not receive adequate pension benefits upon retirement. Moreover, earlier retirement provisions for women may actually dissuade employers from hiring them. Furthermore, employers may be reluctant to finance professional training for women under the assumption that their period of productivity will be shorter than that of men, thus lessening their chances of accessing positions with greater responsibility. Finally, early retirement may hinder the progress of career-oriented women because they may not stay long enough in the job.

Governments may wish to rethink pension policies with a view to achieving the right balance to encourage gender equity in recruitment, covering men's and women's financial needs at retirement age, and ensuring sustainability of the pension system. Spending less time in paid work affects women's career profiles and earnings; it leads to gender disparities in the workplace, in the labour market and in old age. At the same time, coverage of women through their husbands' pensions raises the question of whether a link exists between pension practices and informality, where women are over-represented. The absence of pension benefits may affect married women and single or divorced women very differently, with the latter experiencing higher poverty and having no way of seizing work opportunities if not helped by family members.

Policy makers could also consider various measures to help women understand the pitfalls of working less, including awareness-raising campaigns, information centres, special programmes for rural women who lack access to information, and spaces on government web sites dedicated to women's pensions.

Box 4.8. **The European Court of Justice and different pensionable ages**

According to the global Women's Economic Opportunity Index, 51 economies recommended different retirement ages for women and men in 2010, and 13 actually made it mandatory to retire at a specific age. Since women typically live longer but have lower savings than men, these laws can cause or exacerbate women's poverty in old age. In two rulings in 2008 and 2009, the European Court of Justice found that different pensionable ages for male and female civil servants in Greece and Italy violated the principles of equal pay. Both governments responded by reforming their pension laws to eliminate this discrimination by 2013.

Source: UN Women, 2011, *Progress of the World's Women: In Pursuit of Justice.*

Regarding income taxes, regulations in the six countries are gender neutral in principle, and revenues are taxed on an individual basis. But in practice there can be advantages for men. If child tax incentives exist, they primarily benefit the "head of the family", which, as noted previously, refers to women only in exceptional cases.

- In **Libya**,[94] **Morocco**[95] and **Tunisia**,[96] tax allowances are granted to the husband even if his wife earns a salary and contributes to child-related and household expenses. A taxpaying woman will not benefit from these allowances unless she proves that she is providing a living for her husband and children.
- In **Egypt**, every taxpayer is considered independently, which allows all taxpayers to benefit from the same tax deductions.[97]
- In **Jordan**, husband and wife may opt to file their income taxes jointly, but this does not affect the tax base.[98]
- In **Algeria**, each taxpayer is taxable on both his personal income and that of his children and those persons living with him and considered dependent.[99]

These very preliminary observations on income taxes warrant further examination. They seem to indicate that the system is neutral, whereas tax allowances in relation to children favour men. The systems as designed are not discriminatory but they may, in combination with other provisions and social norms, negatively affect married women's decisions to enter the formal workforce. Taxation of their revenues, which are probably smaller than those of their husbands in light of the general observations concerning recruitment, career development and wages, may be considered high and thus dissuade women's formal involvement in the economy as employees and entrepreneurs.

Governments may consider determining whether and to what extent their tax systems support the withdrawal of women from the labour market or encourage them to work informally. In particular, people from the poorer social groups may turn to informal labour in order to meet their immediate financial needs without the burden of taxation, while at the same time excluding themselves from social benefits like pensions that would help them provide for the future.

Entrepreneurship

Legislation on the establishment and management of businesses in the six countries does not distinguish between men and women. But the fact that entrepreneurship is far less frequent among women than men, as seen in Chapter 1, suggests that women may face additional challenges. Work experience and business contacts, which are limited for many women, are critical for business success: the businesses of women with prior work experience generally have a higher chance of survival. Legal provisions and social practices may also affect the ability of women to establish and develop an enterprise.

Accessing bank finance

Article 13 of CEDAW expressly requires that women have equal access to family benefits and forms of financial credit, including mortgages.

All six countries guarantee access to funding to both sexes under the same conditions. The general matrimonial regime of separate property means that the wife is in principle able to administer those assets and dispose of them freely, but as seen in Chapter 3, family law and cultural norms influence women's wealth. Women often have fewer personal assets than men, whether due to lower levels of formal work experience, lower wage income, smaller inheritances for daughters than for sons, or less land or household property, and this influences their ability to secure a loan through collateral.

Data on business funding is limited, and much evidence on access to financial support for starting or developing a business comes through discussions with women entrepreneurs. One noteworthy element is women's lower access to bank accounts, credit cards and debit cards (Figure 4.1). Overall, only 18% of the population in the MENA region has an account with a financial institution, and for women this figure drops to 13% (IMF, 2013). Disparities exist among countries. The share of Algerian women holding an account at a financial institution is four times higher than in Egypt, although since 2011 the share of women with a bank account has increased sharply in both countries, by 50% and 40%, respectively. In Jordan, over the same period, the number of women with bank accounts decreased by 10%. Women's restricted involvement with the banking system, which may notably be linked to the level and nature of assets owned, may limit their financial education as they are insufficiently exposed to financial operations. Furthermore, their reduced involvement may have a bearing on their credit history. This, in turn, may affect the capacity of female small-business owners to raise funds to expand their businesses.

Figure 4.1. **Access to finance by gender, 2013 (%)**

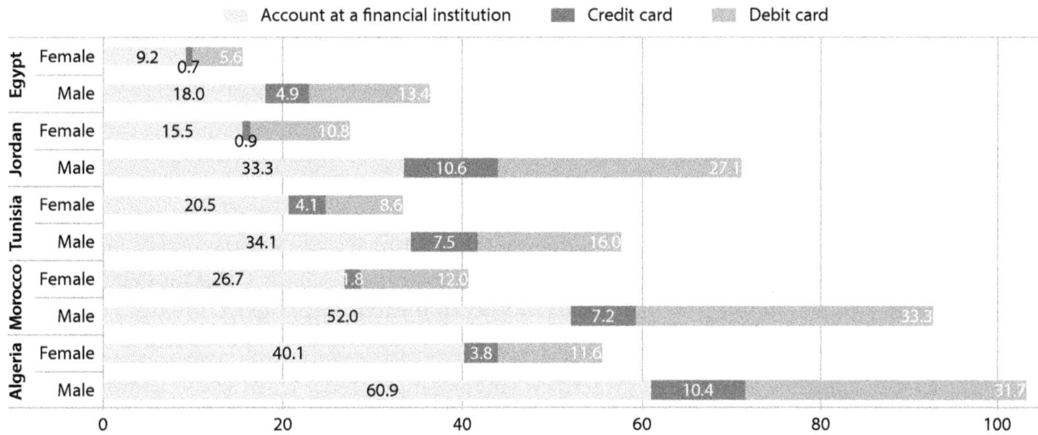

Source: World Bank (2015), World Bank Entrepreneurial Statistics 2015, http://data.worldbank.org/.

Note: Values for Morocco from 2011.

Debt financing is a principal external source of financing for entrepreneurs in the MENA region. Nevertheless, banks in the region are particularly prudent and risk averse. Access to finance through commercial loans and project financing is a major obstacle because it typically requires collateral, which is limited to immovable assets. Lack of sufficient collateral is a key obstacle for women and hence limits their access to resources and funds. Women are more likely to own moveable assets, such as jewellery, which are rarely acceptable as collateral for business loans (World Bank, 2013). Poor individuals often lack the formal property rights required to translate their property into capital and hence collateral (De Soto, 1997).

Table 4.3. **Percentage of adults who borrowed money from a financial institution in the past year (2014)**

	Total	Male	Female
Algeria	2.2	1.3	3.0
Egypt	6.3	7.6	4.9
Jordan	13.6	16.7	10.3
Morocco	4.3	5.0	3.6
Tunisia	8.0	9.9	6.2

Source: Union of Arab Banks research based on World Bank (2014), World Bank Global Financial Inclusion Database 2014.

Note: Values for Morocco from 2011.

Bank lending practices may require women to involve their husband as a co-signer. In Egypt and Jordan, for instance, certain banks demand the husband's consent when his wife applies for a loan.

In support of women's entrepreneurship development and to facilitate access to funds, governments could establish a guarantee mechanism to act as the applicant's guarantor and thereby encourage private funding, such as bank loans. By guaranteeing the loan, the government would ensure that if the debtor was unable to fulfil the obligations, it would take over the debt. Through this mechanism the risk of default is lower, making the bank more likely to issue the loan.

Box 4.9. **Morocco's financing mechanisms in support of women entrepreneurship**

To support the financing of enterprises run by women, Morocco's Central Guarantee Fund (*Caisse centrale de garantie*, CCG) teamed up with the Ministry of Economy and Finance in March 2013 to launch a guarantee tool called "*Ilayki*" ("towards you"). The guarantee covers 80% of bank loans of up to MAD 1 million (Moroccan dirham, about EUR 100 000) that are granted to women, and was able to help around 50 businesses within the first year.

Ilayki was launched through an awareness campaign involving caravans in communities around the country to inform women entrepreneurs about the availability of financing through the CCG (carried out in partnership with the Association of Women Entrepreneurs of Morocco). The CCG also developed agreements with banks to promote the guarantees. Along with the guarantee, the CCG helps women identify their business needs and develop their financing file, and it accompanies them through the process with the banks.

In addition, the National Agency for Promotion of SMEs (Maroc PME) implemented a Women Business Financing project that included efforts to sensitise financial institutions to the needs of women clients, for example recommending that banks engage in gender-sensitivity training for their front office staff. Access to commercial bank credit is still difficult, but some banks have initiated targeted marketing campaigns to reach out to the women's market.

Alternative funding

In practice, women rely more on personal and family resources than on bank loans. It is noteworthy that both men and women in the six countries borrow most from family and friends, an indicator of the shortcomings of formal financial institutions (Table 4.4). Borrowing from friends or family is highest in Morocco and lowest in Algeria and Tunisia.

Table 4.4. **Borrowing by source, 2014 (%)**

	Financial institution	Private informal lender	Family or friends
Algeria	2.2	1.5	13.2
Egypt	6.3	2.5	21.5
Jordan	13.6	1.1	17.4
Morocco	4.3	1.9	40.9
Tunisia	8.0	3.3	16.1

Source: World Bank Global Financial Inclusion Database 2014.

Note: Values for Morocco from 2011.

Another source of funding is microcredit, the lending of small amounts to low-income clients who traditionally lack access to banking and related services. It is a lever for social inclusion: low-income persons who are normally excluded from the traditional banking sector can gain access to the financial resources necessary to start and develop self-employment activities that generate revenues. Microfinance, which is rather well-developed in the region, spread because banks outsourced this customer segment and because non-governmental organisations (NGOs) created microcredit institutions. Microloan initiatives undeniably are a precious development tool, though they also have limitations. In taking on high interest rates, women risk becoming over-indebted. In Tunisia, for instance, the focus group noted that women feared putting their family in danger if their business failed and they were left with debts.

Box 4.10. **Support of women's businesses through microfinance**

Morocco has enacted legislation on microcredit and provides support for microcredit associations to make financing more readily available to women who are unable to qualify for credit from conventional banks.*

In **Algeria**, the National Microcredit Management Agency offers a microcredit programme that prioritises home-based work, trades and handicrafts, particularly among the female population. It offers interest-free loans for the purchase of raw materials, and women represent almost 63% of those benefiting from this measure. In addition to these financial services, female entrepreneurs involved in the microcredit programme have also received non-financial benefits such as training and coaching (CEDAW, 2012: 23).

In **Tunisia**, the Tunisian Solidarity Bank has created a low-interest line of credit for NGOs active in this area as part of a new microcredit programme targeting low-income people and families capable of starting an economic activity. Women benefit from 31.3% of the projects financed and 26% of the amounts allocated (CEDAW, 2009: 46).

In **Jordan**, the Microfund for Women finances and expands small enterprises and reaches out to the needy in disadvantaged areas. Women represent 97% of beneficiaries. The fund also offers non-financial services, such as education, business development, social services, capacity building, incentive programmes and insurance to cover year-round and seasonal financing. The Jordanian Hashemite Fund for Human Development also provides revolving loans at low interest and with convenient repayment terms to women's associations and rural women to support productive family enterprises (CEDAW, 2006: 43).

* For examples of such initiatives, see CEDAW (2006), p. 46 et seq.

When a company expands, its financing needs increase and may exceed microcredit ceilings. In this case, a company may need access to bank financing or alternative funding sources. But a woman's credit history maybe insufficient to expand her business if her previous borrowing was on a small scale.

The fact that women raise less external financing than men can stifle the potential of their enterprises to innovate, grow, develop new products and services, hire skilled employees and access international markets.

Alternative financing sources are emerging in the region. Venture capital, private equity, grants, venture debt, convertible debt and angel investment are sources of funding for high-growth and innovative enterprises. They could, in certain circumstances, be promising alternatives for women entrepreneurs who lack collateral.

Business climate

From a legal perspective, men and women enjoy the same possibilities when it comes to business registration and development. As soon as they reach the age of majority, women are allowed to sign any type of business contract.

Improving business environments is among the foremost priorities for nurturing the private sector in the MENA region. Regulatory burdens have a disproportionate impact on micro, small and medium-sized enterprises (MSMEs) by diverting scarce resources to compliance with regulations and administrative procedures; they may discourage setting up and developing a business or integrating a business into the formal economy.

Although business registration and licensing procedures are gender neutral, they are more complicated to manage for women. Structures supportive of women's entrepreneurship are insufficient, and information on access to finance and markets is scarce. Women entrepreneurs are faced with specific obstacles and constraints that stem from both the demand side (use of finance and business development services) and the supply side (bank lending practices and the range of business-development services and incubators available and sensitive to women's needs). Lack of work experience, limited access to networks and a lack of safe transportation can also present obstacles for women. Gender-neutral business registration and licensing procedures are more complicated to manage for women, including because of red tape, corruption and accessibility of services. Women may indeed also experience more difficulties reaching the institutions responsible of the administrative procedures. Many companies created by women are part of the informal sector; they are not registered and may run no accounting system.

Participants in focus groups reported that in addition to financial and administrative difficulties, women can face resistance from their own families. The husband's supremacy in marital relations affects women's economic autonomy and decision making on launching a business of their own, even in countries where they do not need the husband's authorisation in principle. This support is essential, as women entrepreneurs' strongest backing may be from their husbands and families, as many testimonies confirm. The groups also mentioned stress and social pressures as major hindrances to female entrepreneurship, especially in rural environments, where a woman who goes out to work runs the risk of damaging her reputation regardless of what she does.

Nonetheless, an increasing number of wives of men who are unemployed or on low incomes, as well as widows and divorced women, are setting up their own businesses in the region. Focus group participants noted the need for policies to raise awareness of entrepreneurship as a career option for women. Programmes are also needed to boost self-esteem. Entrepreneurship networks can be a major source of knowledge, role models and experience sharing.

Safety in public and at work

Violence against women undermines their agency and potential to act freely in the economic sphere. Worldwide, the first form of violence against women is domestic, but violence and harassment also exist in the public space and at work. All forms of violence limit women's capacity to engage in the economy and affect their productivity.

In 1992, the CEDAW Committee qualified gender-based violence as a type of discrimination within the meaning of Article 1 of the Convention, and stated: "Equality in employment can be seriously impaired when women are subjected to gender-specific violence, such as sexual harassment in the workplace" (CEDAW, 1992). ILO standards[100] also require a violence-free working environment where women can feel secure. The ILO Committee of Experts on the Application of Conventions and Recommendations considers sexual harassment to be prohibited by the 1958 Convention Concerning Discrimination in Respect of Employment and Occupation (ILO, 1996). It declared that sexual harassment undermines equality at the workplace by calling into question individual integrity and the well-being of workers, damaging working relationships and impairing productivity.[101]

The six countries under review have recently introduced legislation into the penal code sanctioning sexual harassment and/or have made it an offence under the labour code.

- In **Egypt**, any gesture, words or inappropriate sexual or pornographic behaviour has been punishable since 2014, when the penal law was amended by presidential decree.[102] When sexual harassment is proven, the offender will be punished with a fine and a prison term of not less than one year.[103] A clause was also introduced on harassment at the workplace, stipulating a more severe sentence for an offender who is in a position of authority over the victim. The labour law addresses sexual harassment in the private sector.
- In **Morocco**, persons who abuse their position of authority to harass somebody with the intent of receiving sexual favours have since 2003 been punishable under the penal code with one or two years of prison as well as a fine.[104] The labour code considers sexual harassment of an employee by his or her employer an incitement to debauchery and as a serious offence; accordingly when an employee resigns because of such acts, the termination of her employment is deemed to be dismissal without reasonable cause.[105]
- In **Tunisia**, the penal code has punished sexual harassment since 2004.[106] Any individual who harasses another through humiliating or offensive acts, words or gestures intended to cause the victim to submit to one's own sexual overtures or to those of a third party is subject to a fine and imprisonment for one year.[107] This text has a general application and does not take into account the specificities of professional relations.
- In **Algeria**, imprisonment of two months to one year and a fine were introduced into the penal code in 2004 for those who abuse their authority by giving orders, threatening, imposing constraints or exerting pressure on another person to obtain sexual favours.[108] A 2015 law also introduced the concept of harassment in public places.[109]
- In **Jordan**, the labour code since 2008 has authorised an employee who has been a victim of harassment to terminate her employment contract and obtain full compensation.[110] An employer harassing a female employee can be sentenced to pay her damages and interest. The Ministry of Employment may also decide to close the establishment if this type of abuse is repeated. Moreover, the Civil Services Statute of 2007 deems sexual harassment in public service to be an offence against honour.
- In **Libya**, the labour code authorises an employee subject to sexual harassment to resign from her job and still maintain her rights to end-of-employment compensation.[111]

These legislative provisions mark progress and are in line with the countries' international commitments to combat sexual harassment against women. However, the provisions often incriminate sexual harassment only by the employer and not yet by fellow employees or customers.

Sexual harassment can be a direct or indirect deterrent to women's economic empowerment, as families may discourage women from working due to the perceived dangers. In a 2013 survey by UN Women in Egypt, fully 99% of the women and girls who were interviewed said they had experienced some form of sexual harassment.[112] It is also worth noting that while women may be exposed to physical or psychological violence without sexual intent, this is not explicitly addressed, although ILO standards[113] require a violence-free working environment where women and men can feel safe.

The fact that legal protections against sexual harassment have limitations arose in discussions in focus groups. Participants noted that women are often unaware of the existence of the laws, as well as the reluctance of officials to implement such laws. They also noted that women rarely report workplace harassment out of shame or fear that society may label them as "immodest". Violence in the workplace is thus generally kept secret; victims fear reprisals such as dismissal, social stigma and family tensions. During discussions, one victim explained that she had had to leave her job to end harassment, but had refused to bring it up. Another testimony concerned relations with clients, who often seek favours during external meetings outside of office hours. An ILO sexual harassment prevention awareness project in Jordan is an initiative that might warrant consideration in other countries and industries (Box 4.11).

Box 4.11. **ILO initiative to raise awareness of sexual harassment in Jordan's garment factories**

In 2011, allegations were made of widespread rape being committed against workers at one of Jordan's largest clothing factories. Although the allegations were not substantiated, reports of unwanted sexual advances towards workers are common across the global garment-manufacturing sector. The ILO's investigation of the situation in Jordan found that many workers had very little understanding of what constitutes sexual harassment, even though they were concerned about it. As a result, the ILO launched a sexual-harassment awareness project with several factories, training workers, supervisors and senior management on how to identify, prevent and report instances of sexual harassment. ILO advisers also worked with senior management in these factories to put into place policies and procedures that allow workers to report sexual harassment and seek redress. More information is available at: http://betterwork.org/jordan/.

Source: ILO (2014), *Labour Inspection, Gender Equality and Non-Discrimination in the Arab States*, Beirut.

Harassment of women also occurs frequently on the way to work. This infringes on their rights and creates barriers to their entry into the labour market. Algeria, Egypt and Tunisia punish sexual harassment in public places as a criminal offence. But discussions revealed that, in practice, female victims of violence in public places do not usually press charges due to social and cultural pressure. Instead they avoid mobility. Irregular service, a lack of street lighting and an overall lack of safety also limit women's travel and reduce their freedom of movement for professional reasons. These factors diminish their chances of finding or keeping a job, particularly in remote areas. Women's involvement in the economy clearly depends on their ability to reach the workplace safely and quickly. Public transport and infrastructure are of primary importance and play an obvious role in women's employment options.

This was illustrated in a focus group discussion among young women, who said that even though families tended to agree with their working for financial reasons, acceptance sometimes depended on the proximity of the workplace to home. With families concerned about safety when young women need to wait for public transport in unlit and/or remote areas, preference is given to daytime jobs near the home if the family lacks a car. Because women often get around on foot in rural areas, they turn down jobs further away. Participants identified the lack of safe public transport as a barrier to their mobility.

Although the constitutions of most of the countries under review guarantee women freedom of movement, women nonetheless may face limitations on their mobility as employees or entrepreneurs. Factors include the location of the family home, which is chosen by the husband, and the need for women in some countries to obtain their husband's or father's permission to travel (see Chapter 2). Lack of mobility may also affect the development or growth of the businesses of women entrepreneurs. They take transportation and infrastructure security into account, and may confine themselves to activities requiring less movement or travel, particularly in remote areas.

Improving transportation and infrastructure to support greater mobility would have a positive impact on women's capacity to undertake a wider variety of economic activities and would allow them to conduct their businesses more efficiently.

Box 4.12. **Moving beyond women-only buses**

Women-only public transportation is currently available in various countries, including Brazil, India, Indonesia, Japan, Malaysia, Mexico, Nepal and Thailand. But some specialists on urban transport argue that cities need to move beyond women-only buses by raising awareness within communities on the need to end sexual harassment in public transport.

Bianca Bianchi Alves, an urban transport specialist, and Karla Dominguez Gonzalez, a gender specialist, have described a World Bank project in Mexico City, where harassment in public transport is so extensive, they say, that 65% of women suffer from gender-based violence in transit vehicles and public spaces related to transportation. They write:

"The project, called *Hazme el Paro* (an informal way of saying 'help' or 'have my back'), has involved local and international feminist organisations, specialists in social norms and behaviour change, app developers and urban transport organisations such as Embarq and the Institute for Transportation and Development Policy. While this project is being implemented as a pilot for now, there is an evaluation component conducted by George Washington University that will help support the design of a larger-scale project. A local transport company has signed on to help with the pilot phase, by agreeing to implement interventions in some of its buses.

The strategy consists of three main interventions:

- A marketing campaign that creates a sense of community and states a strong, united opposition to sexual harassment against women,
- A smartphone app to facilitate reporting and improve diagnosis, and
- A consistent awareness community training on non-confrontational ways of stopping harassment in public transport.

These trainings include bus drivers and operators, police and civil society in general."

Source: Blanca Bianchi Alves and Karla Dominguez González (2015), *Smart measures in transport: Moving beyond women's-only buses*, World Bank Blogs.

Conclusions

The labour codes of the six countries provide for non-discrimination on the basis of gender and for equal pay for women and men. No difference is made in principle between men and women on social protection, though non-wage employment benefits tend to be payable to married men.

The labour codes restrict women's activities at night and in hazardous work; this reinforces the concept that women are vulnerable and need to be protected. International standards have for some time advocated gender-neutral provisions in order to allow women to decide for themselves on whether they need protection and to increase the recruitment pool and extend women's job opportunities, including female entrepreneurship.

Labour codes provide for maternity leave, nursing of new-borns and parental leave for mothers. Provisions are more advantageous in the public sector, while private-sector employers often have to cover associated expenses and provide childcare facilities. Such expenses may be significant for small businesses, which may seek to avoid bearing such costs by limiting the recruitment of women. Flexible time and part-time work are rare in the private sector and are generally available for women only. Women are also able to retire earlier than men when in formal employment. Testimonies indicate that these different provisions seem to reinforce gender stereotypes and limit women's recruitment and promotion.

Income tax, business laws and legislation on access to funding are gender neutral, but women entrepreneurs may confront more hurdles then men when setting up and growing a business, notably due to socio-economic conditions and norms, which are indirectly triggered or reinforced by personal status laws. This can result for women in reduced work experience, limited assets, concerns about family support and security, and worries about social perceptions.

The governments of the six countries have made progress in adopting legislative provisions on sexual harassment in line with their international commitments, although women may face other forms of violence in public life or at work. Improving infrastructure and transportation facilities would support women's mobility and access to the labour market and services.

An examination of the different provisions concerning women's labour rights indicates that not all governments are fully in line with international standards and best practices. To support women's economic empowerment and integration, governments may consider revisiting the relevant provisions and examine, notably in light of the equality provisions adopted in their respective constitutions, how to enhance equality between women and men and to develop systems supporting stronger participation of women in the workforce and as entrepreneurs. They may also test whether and to what extent the interaction of labour-related provisions with unequal bargaining power in the household, pursuant to the personal status laws, may push women out of the labour market and possibly into informality.

When contemplating such revisions, states may seek to strengthen the input of employer and labour associations and consider developing bargaining mechanisms on issues related to the terms and conditions of employment, including wages and benefits, skills development and representation in organisations.

Recommendations

Governments are encouraged to:

- Combat gender-related discrimination against women in all types and sectors of work and throughout all stages of their working life, including recruitment, access to promotion and senior management positions, and pay relative to male colleagues; apply international standards concerning the jobs from which women are restricted (so-called "hazardous" jobs or jobs with night hours); strengthen monitoring and sanctioning mechanisms to bridge existing gaps between labour laws and practices.
- Ensure that the labour code covers all categories of workers, all types of work and all sectors in order to reduce informality and protect all employees, and in particular women.
- Review maternity leave and child care provisions to dissociate the perceived costs of childrearing from women as much as possible: ensure that employers do not bear maternity leave or childcare costs directly by offering publicly supported, indirect financing mechanisms (e.g. social insurance funds) and state-supported childcare solutions; reform tax and social-benefits systems to provide equal financial incentives for both parents to work; promote equal sharing of family responsibilities through parental leaves in line with ILO recommendations.
- Enact regulations and/or provide incentives for employers to support part-time employment, remote working and flexible hours for both genders in order to help reconcile working hours and family life.
- Guarantee women a safe environment at and on their way to work by: ensuring strict enforcement of sexual harassment regulations and punishing offenders; allowing victims to leave their jobs if desired while maintaining their rights to dismissal compensation; penalising harassment in public places; and enhancing women's mobility by improving transportation and infrastructure.
- Foster a greater role for women in economic decision making through affirmative-action programmes or measures such as temporary quotas or targets in public and private governance structures, e.g. leadership and management positions as well as company-board positions; complement such measures by leadership-development opportunities for women and men to give equal access to senior posts through career counselling services, coaching and mentoring.
- Reduce barriers to women's entrepreneurship through policies that: support equal access to finance, including the amendment of current legislation; prohibit discrimination based on sex or marital status; foster the development of credit registries and credit bureaus; encourage financial institutions to take different sorts of collateral into consideration; develop guarantee mechanisms to compensate for women's limited assets; support the development of alternative funding sources; and increase women's financial education.
- Move towards pension-age parity (public/private and by gender) by encouraging female employees to prolong the age at which they retire so that they may build up longer contribution periods; launch awareness-raising campaigns, information centres, special programmes for rural women and spaces dedicated to women's pensions on government web sites to help women understand the implications for their pensions of working less than full time or retiring early.

Notes

1. See ILO Convention concerning Discrimination in Respect of Employment and Occupation, ILO Equal Remuneration Convention (Article 2) and CEDAW Article 11.
2. Article 5 bis, added to the 1966 Labour Law by a Law of 1993.
3. Article 11 of the 1983 Ordinance concerning general statutes for employees of the state, local government and public administrative bodies. This provision could apply to guards in male prisons.
4. Article 4 of the 2007 Civil Service Regulation.
5. The absence of such a provision was noted by the ILO Committee of Experts in its observations on Jordan in 2013 (ILO, CEACR, Discrimination (Employment and Occupation) Convention, Observation to Jordan, 2013, www.ilo.org/dyn/normlex/en/f?p=1000:13100:0::NO:13100:P13100_COMMENT_ID,P11110_COUNTRY_ID,P11110_COUNTRY_NAME,P11110_COMMENT_YEAR:3145506,103201,Jordan,2013.
6. Article 21 of the 2010 Labour Relations Law.
7. Article 6 para. 3 of the 1990 Labour Relations Law.
8. Article 9 of the 2003 Labour Law.
9. Articles 35 of Labour Law No. 12/2003.
10. CSR and Gender, http://schemaadvisory.com/wp-content/uploads/2014/12/CIDA-Final-Short.pdf.
11. Articles 17 and 84 of the 1990 Labour Relations Law.
12. Article 35 of the 2003 Labour Law.
13. Article 21 of the 2010 Labour Relations Law.
14. Article 9 of the 2003 Labour Law.
15. See, for instance, ILO, Equal Remuneration Convention, Observation on Egypt, www.ilo.org/dyn/normlex/en/f?p=1000:13100:0::NO:13100:P13100_COMMENT_ID,P11110_COUNTRY_ID,P11110_COUNTRY_NAME,P11110_COMMENT_YEAR:3058256,102915,Egypt,2012
16. Article 69 of the 2016 Algerian Constitution.
17. Article 17 of the 2014 Egyptian Constitution.
18. Article 23 of the 1952 Jordanian Constitution.
19. Article 8 of the 2011 Libyan Constitutional Declaration.
20. Article 31 of the 2011 Moroccan Constitution.
21. Article 38 of the 2014 Tunisian Constitution.
22. Social Insurance Law of 1975.
23. Article 6 of the Social Security Law.
24. Article 8 of the 2004 Civil Health Insurance System.
25. Article 81 of the 2014 Social Security Law.
26. Law of 1983 on Social Insurance as amended and its executive regulations.
27. Article 25(b) of the Civil Service Regulations of 2007.
28. Article 2 of the 2013 Law.
29. Article 40 of the Dahir of 1972 on the Social Security Regime as amended in 2004.

30. Law of 1994 and Decree of 1995.

31. The 1948 Night Work (Women) Convention (Revised) obliged ratifying states to prohibit women from working in industrial undertakings at night. It was replaced by the 1990 Convention concerning Night Work, which applies to all workers regardless of sex. Night work refers to "all work which is performed during a period of not less than seven consecutive hours, including the interval from midnight to 5 a.m."

32. ILO 1935 Convention concerning the Employment of Women on Underground Work in Mines of all Kinds (Article 2) provided that, in principle, no female of any age should be employed in underground work in mines. In 1995 the Convention concerning Safety and Health in Mines was adopted to provide equal protection of all employees in mines.

33. Article 89 of the 2003 Labour Code.

34. 1996 Decree of the Minister of Labour.

35. Article 66 of the 1966 Labour Law.

36. Article 27 of the 1990 Labour Relations Law.

37. Article 96 of the 2010 Labour Relations Law.

38. Article 171 of the 2003 Labour Law.

39. Article 174 of the 2003 Labour Law

40. Article 90 of the 2003 Labour Law.

41. Article 181 of the Labour Law.

42. Article 179 of the Labour Law.

43. Article 77 of the 2003 Labour Law.

44. 1996 Decree of the Minister of Labour concerning the jobs and hours in which the employment of women is prohibited.

45. Article 1 of the 2003 Ministerial Decree determining the work for which women may not be employed.

46. Article 78 of the 1966 Labour Law.

47. Article 24 of the 2010 Labour Relations Law.

48. Article 23 of the 1952 Jordanian Constitution.

49. Article 68 of the 1966 Labour Law.

50. Article 3 of the 2004 Decree.

51. Article 5 of the 2003 Ministerial Decree. The prohibition does not extend to women in administrative supervisory or technical positions.

52. Article 29 of the 1990 Labour Relations Law.

53. Article 89 of the 2003 Labour Law and 2003 Ministerial Decree.

54. 1996 Decree of the Minister of Labour.

55. Article 96 of the 2010 Labour Relations Law.

56. Article 159 of the 2003 Moroccan Labour Law, Articles 20 and 68.4 of the 1966 Tunisian Labour Law.

57. Article 120 of the 2003 Labour Law and Article 92 of the 2003 Labour Law.

58. Article 27(a)(1) of the 1996 Labour Law.

59. Article 25 of Law No. 12 on Labour Regulations, www.ilo.org/dyn/travail/docs/2079/Law%20No.%2012%20for%202010%20concerning%20of%20labor%20relations.pdf.

60. ILO Recommendation No. 191 suggests that maternity leave should be at least 18 weeks.

61. Article 91 of the 2003 Labour Law. The previous Labour Code required six months only. In practice, employers seem to take advantage of this article by concluding contracts limited to less than 10 months. Moreover, if a female employee gets married during the contract period, usually the contract is not renewed (Lohmann, 2010).

62. Article 64 of the 1966 Labour Law provides for extension with a medical certificate by 15-day periods, up to a maximum of 12 weeks.

63. Art. 78 (new) of the 1960 law regarding the organisation of social security regimes, as amended in 1970.

64. Article 48 of the 1983 Law concerning general statutes for employees of the state, local government and public administrative bodies.

65. Article 212 of the 2006 Public Officials Status Law and Article 54 of the Labour Relations Law.

66. Article 269 of the 2003 Labour Law.

67. Article 122 of the 1966 Labour Law and Article 31 of the Collective Convention as amended in 1985 (private sector). Article 40 para. 4 of the 1983 Ordinance on Civil Servants concerning general statutes for employees of the state, local government and public administrative bodies.

68. The previous ILO Maternity Convention, adopted in 1919, specified two half-hour nursing breaks.

69. Article 161 of the 2003 Labour Law for the private sector and 1958 Ordinance on public servants for the public sector.

70. Article 71 of the 1996 Labour Law. The 2007 Civil Service Regulation does not grant a similar right, and management has discretion on whether to allow a mother to take an hour off to nurse her infant.

71. Article 64 of the 1966 Labour Law and Article 48 bis of the 1983 Ordinance on Civil Servants concerning general statutes for employees of the state, local government and public administrative bodies (for a maximum of six months).

72. Article 25 of the 2010 Labour Relations Law.

73. Article 93 of the 2003 Labour Law.

74. Article 214 of the 2006 Public Officials Status Law.

75. Article 72 of the 1978 Law 48. During the leave, the state shall pay its quota and that of the female employee in the social insurance subscription, or pay the employee an indemnity equivalent to 25% of her salary.

76. Article 94 of the 2003 Labour Law.

77. Article 108(a)(5) of the 2007 Civil Service Regulation.

78. Article 67 of the 1996 Labour Law.

79. Article 156 of the 2003 Labour Law.

80. Article 48 of the 1983 Ordinance on Civil Servants concerning general statutes for employees of the state, local government and public administrative bodies.

81. Article 72 of the 1996 Labour Law.

82. Article 162 of the 2003 Labour Law.

83. Article 96 of the 2003 Labour Law.

84. Article 26 of 2010 Labour Relations Law.

85. ILO Part-Time Work Convention, 1994, and Recommendations.

86. 1990 Labour Relations Law and Executive Decree of 1997 on part-time work.

87. Articles 10 and 11 of the 1997 Executive Decree on part-time work.

88. Executive Decrees of 1997 (CEDAW, 2010b).

89. Article 72 of the 1978 State Civil Servants Law.

90. Implementing regulations of the 2010 Labour Relations Law.

91. Article 94.2-94.14 of the 1966 Labour Law.

92. ILO 1967 Invalidity, Old-Age and Survivors' Benefits Convention, Article 15.

93. Article 18.

94. Law of 2010 on Taxation of Income.

95. Article 74 of the Taxes Law of 2006.

96. Article 40 of the Law on Taxation of Individual Incomes.

97. Law No. 91 of 2005.

98. Articles 9 and 17 of the Income Tax Law of 2014.

99. Law 90-36 from 31/12/1990 relative to the financial law 1991.

100. See for instance ILO code of practice, *Workplace violence in services sectors and measures to combat this phenomenon*, 2004.

101. The Committee defined sexual harassment as "any insult or inappropriate remark, joke, insinuation and comment on a person's dress, physique, age, family situation, etc.; a condescending or paternalistic attitude with sexual implications undermining dignity; any unwelcome invitation or request, implicit or explicit, whether or not accompanied by threats; any lascivious look or other gesture associated with sexuality; and any unnecessary physical contact such as touching, caresses, pinching or assault." (Ibid.)

102. With at least six months of imprisonment and/or a fine of EGP 3 000 to 5 000 (Egyptian pounds). The sentence can be stiffened to up to one year of imprisonment and EGP 10 000 to 20 000 if the harassment is carried out with intent to obtain sexual favours.

103. Presidential Decree of 2014 amending Articles 306 bis A and 306 bis B of the Penal Code.

104. Article 503-1 of the Criminal Law.

105. Article 40 of the 2003 Labour Law.

106. Article 226ter of the Criminal Law, as amended in 2004.

107. Ibid.

108. Article 341 bis of the Penal Law, added in 2004.

109. Law of 5 March 2015 amending the Criminal Law.

110. Article 29 of the 1996 Labour Law, as amended in 2008.

111. Article 12 of the 2010 Labour Relations Law.

112. The study is based on a sample of 2 332 girls and women, and 1 168 boys and men, aged 10-35, in the governorates of Cairo, Alexandria, Dakahlia, Gharbia, Ismailia, Assiut, and Qena. See: UN Women, "Study on ways and methods to eliminate sexual harassment in Egypt", *UN Reports*, 23 May 2013, http://harassmap.org/en/wp-content/uploads/2014/02/287_Summaryreport_eng_low-1.pdf.

113. See for instance, ILO code of practice, *Workplace violence in services sectors and measures to combat this phenomenon*, 2004.

References

ADB (2013), *Kazakhstan Country Gender Assessment*, Asian Development Bank, Philippines, www.adb.org/sites/default/files/institutional-document/34051/files/kazakhstan-country-gender-assessment.pdf.

Addati, L., N. Cassirer and K. Gilchrist (2014), *Maternity and Paternity at Work: Law and Practice Across the World*, International Labour Office, Geneva, http://ilo.org/wcmsp5/groups/public/---dgreports/---dcomm/---publ/documents/publication/wcms_242615.pdf.

Albanesi, S. and C. Olivetti (2006), "Home production, market production and the gender wage gap: Incentives and expectations," *National Bureau of Economic Research Working Paper Series,* No. 12212, NBER, Cambridge, Massachusetts, http://dx.doi.org/10.1016/j.red.2008.08.001.

Anderson, K.H., J.E. Foster and D.E. Frisvold (2010), "Investing in health: The long-term impact of Head Start on smoking", *Economic Inquiry,* Vol. 48/3, pp. 587-602, Eugene, Oregon, http://onlinelibrary.wiley.com/doi/10.1111/j.1465-7295.2008.00202.x/epdf.

Barsoum, G. (2010), "When there is 'no respect' at work: Job quality issues for women in Egypt's private sector", *OIDA International Journal of Sustainable Development,* Vol. 1/1, pp. 67-80, http://papers.ssrn.com/sol3/papers.cfm?abstract_id=1661196.

Belsky, J. et al. (2007), "Are there long-term effects of early childcare?", *Child Development,* Vol. 78/2, pp. 681-701, http://onlinelibrary.wiley.com/doi/10.1111/j.1467-8624.2007.01021.x/pdf.

Bianchi Alves, B. and K. Dominguez González (2015), "Smart measures in transport: Moving beyond women's-only buses", *World Bank Blogs,* World Bank, Washington, DC, http://blogs.worldbank.org/transport/smart-measures-transport-moving-beyond-women-s-only-buses.

Bradley, R.H. and D.L. Vandell (2007), "Child care and the well-being of children", *Archives of Pediatrics and Adolescent Medicine,* Vol. 161/7, pp. 669-76, https://asu.pure.elsevier.com/en/publications/child-care-and-the-well-being-of-children.

CEDAW (2015), "Sixth periodic report of States Parties due in 2016 (Jordan)", UN Committee on the Elimination of Discrimination Against Women (CEDAW), http://tbinternet.ohchr.org/_layouts/treatybodyexternal/Download.aspx?symbolno=CEDAW%2fC%2fJOR%2f6&Lang=en.

CEDAW (2012), "List of issues and questions with regard to the consideration of periodic reports: Algeria", UN Committee on the Elimination of Discrimination Against Women (CEDAW)m http://repository.un.org/handle/11176/285484.

CEDAW (2010a), "General recommendation No. 28 on the core obligations of States Parties under article 2 of the Convention on the Elimination of All Forms of Discrimination against Women, UN Committee on the Elimination of Discrimination Against Women (CEDAW), http://www2.ohchr.org/english/bodies/cedaw/docs/CEDAW-C-2010-47-GC2.pdf.

CEDAW (2010b), "Combined third and fourth periodic reports of States Parties (Algeria)", UN Committee on the Elimination of Discrimination Against Women (CEDAW), http://tbinternet.ohchr.org/_layouts/treatybodyexternal/Download.aspx?symbolno=CEDAW%2fC%2fDZA%2f3-4&Lang=en.

CEDAW (2010c), "Concluding observations of the Committee on the Elimination of Discrimination against Women (Tunisia)", UN Committee on the Elimination of Discrimination Against Women (CEDAW), p. 10, http://www2.ohchr.org/english/bodies/cedaw/docs/co/CEDAW-C-TUN-CO-6.pdf.

CEDAW (2010d), "Written replies from the government of Tunisia to the list of issues and questions", UN Committee on the Elimination of Discrimination Against Women (CEDAW), http://tbinternet.ohchr.org/_layouts/treatybodyexternal/Download.aspx?symbolno=CEDAW%2fC%2fTUN%2fQ%2f6%2fAdd.1&Lang=en.

CEDAW (2009), "Combined fifth and sixth periodic reports of States Parties (Tunisia)", UN Committee on the Elimination of Discrimination Against Women (CEDAW), p. 39, http://tbinternet.ohchr.org/_layouts/treatybodyexternal/Download.aspx?symbolno=CEDAW%2fC%2fTUN%2f6&Lang=en.

CEDAW (2006), "Consideration of reports submitted by States Parties under Article 18 of the Convention on the Elimination of All Forms of Discrimination against Women", UN Committee on the Elimination of Discrimination Against Women (CEDAW), https://documents-dds-ny.un.org/doc/UNDOC/GEN/N06/563/69/PDF/N0656369.pdf?OpenElement.

CEDAW (2006), "Combined third and fourth reports of States Parties (Jordan)", UN Committee on the Elimination of Discrimination Against Women (CEDAW), http://tbinternet.ohchr.org/_layouts/treatybodyexternal/Download.aspx?symbolno=CEDAW%2fC%2fJOR%2f3-4&Lang=en.

CEDAW (1992), "General recommendation No. 19 (on violence against women)", UN Committee on the Elimination of Discrimination Against Women (CEDAW), www.un.org/womenwatch/daw/cedaw/recommendations/recomm.htm.

CEDAW (1989), "General recommendation No. 12 (on violence against women), UN Committee on the Elimination of Discrimination Against Women (CEDAW), www.un.org/womenwatch/daw/cedaw/recommendations/recomm.htm.

Chichilnisky, G. and E. Hermann Frederiksen (2008), "An equilibrium analysis of the gender wage gap, *International Labour Review* Vol. 147/4, pp. 297–320, Geneva, www.ilo.org/public/english/revue/download/pdf/s1_chichilnisky.pdf.

Cipollone A., E. Patacchini and G. Vallanti (2014), "Female labour market participation in Europe: Novel evidence on trends and shaping factors", *IZA Journal of European Labor Studies*, Vol. 3/18, Bonn, http://repec.iza.org/dp7710.pdf.

Correll, S., S. Benard and I. Paik (2007), "Getting a job: Is there a motherhood penalty?", *American Journal of Sociology*, Vol. 112/5, pp. 1297-1338, www.jstor.org/stable/10.1086/511799.

Del Boca D., S. Pasqua and Ch. Pronzato (2009), "Motherhood and market work decisions in institutional context: A European perspective", *Oxford Economic Papers*, Vol. 61 (suppl. 1), pp. 147-71, http://oep.oxfordjournals.org/content/61/suppl_1/i147.full.pdf.

De Soto, H. (1997), "Dead capital and the poor in Egypt", *Egyptian Centre for Economic Studies Distinguished Lecture Series*, No. 11, Cairo, www.eces.org.eg/Publication.aspx?Id=184.

Destatis (2015), *Statistik zum Elterngeld Beendete Leistungsbezüge für im Jahr 2013 geborene Kinder: Januar 2013 bis März 2015 (*Statistics on parental allowances Completed benefits for children born in 2013: January 2013 to March 2015) (dataset), Statistisches Bundesamt, Wiesbaden, https://www.destatis.de/DE/Publikationen/Thematisch/Soziales/Elterngeld/ElterngeldGeburtenJ_5229201139004.pdf?__blob=publicationFile.

Duncan, G.J. and K. Magnuson (2013), "Investing in preschool programs", *Journal of Economic Perspectives*, Vol. 27/2, pp. 109-32, https://www.aeaweb.org/articles?id=10.1257/jep.27.2.109.

Elgazzar, H. (2015), |Labor market dynamics in Libya: Reintegration for recovery", *World Bank Study*, World Bank, Washington, DC, http://documents.worldbank.org/curated/en/967931468189558835/Labor-market-dynamics-in-Libya-reintegration-for-recovery.

ESCWA (2014), "Access to justice for women and girls in the Arab region: From ratification to implementation of international instruments", *Status of Arab Women Report* United Nations, Beirut, https://www.unescwa.org/sites/www.unescwa.org/files/publications/files/e_escwa_ecw_15_1_e.pdf.

ESCWA (2012), *Addressing Barriers to Women's Economic Participation in the Arab Region*, United Nations, New York, https://www.unescwa.org/sites/www.unescwa.org/files/publications/files/e_escwa_ecw_12_1_e.pdf.

EUROMED (2011), *Access to Justice in the Mediterranean Partner Countries*, Euromed Justice Survey, http://euromed-justiceii.eu/files/site/English_book_Study_Access_to_Justice.pdf.

European Training Foundation (2006), *Technical and Vocational Education and Training in Jordan: Areas for Development Cooperation*, European Communities, Luxembourg, www.etf.europa.eu/pubmgmt.nsf/(getAttachment)/ACE62B7AC28F6695C1257218005884B3/$File/NOTE6V4LW5.pdf.

Fougère D., O. Filatriau and M. To (2014), "Will sooner be better?: The impact of early preschool enrollment on cognitive and noncognitive achievement of children", *CEPR Discussion Papers*, No. 9480, Centre for Economic Policy Research, London, https://ideas.repec.org/p/cpr/ceprdp/9480.html.

Gatti, R. et al. (2013), "Overview", *Free to Prosper: Jobs in the Middle East and North Africa*, World Bank, Washington, DC, http://beta.cmimarseille.org/sites/default/files/AFD/socialprotection/Free%20to%20Prosper%20Jobs%20MENA%20Report%20WB%202013%20Overview.pdf.

GEM (2013), *2012 Women's Report*, Global Entrepreneurship Research Association, London, www.gemconsortium.org/report/48583.

GEM (2012), *2012 GEM Tunisia: National Report*, Global Entrepreneurship Research Association, London, www.gemconsortium.org/report/48801.

Glenn, S., S. Melis and L. Withers (2009), "Gender (in)equality in the labour market: An overview of global trends and developments", International Trade Union Confederation and Income Data Services, Brussels, www.ituc-csi.org/IMG/pdf/GAP-09_EN.pdf.

Görlich, D., I. Stepanok and F. Al-Hussami (2013), "Youth unemployment in Europe and the world: Causes, consequences and solutions" *Kiel Policy Brief*, No. 59, Institute for Word Economy, Kiel, Germany, https://www.ifw-kiel.de/wirtschaftspolitik/zentrum-wirtschaftspolitik/kiel-policy-brief/kpb-2013/KPB_59.pdf.

Hassan, M. and C. Sassanpour (2008), "Labour market pressures in Egypt: Why is the unemployment rate stubbornly high?", *Journal of Development and Economic Policies*, Vol. 10/2, Arab Planning Institute, Kuwait, pp. 79-115, http://adapt.it/adapt-indice-a-z/wp-content/uploads/2014/05/api_labour_market_pressures_2008.pdf.

Havnes T., and M. Mogstad (2011), "No child left behind: Subsidized child care and children's long-run outcomes", *American Economic Journal: Economic Policy*, Vol. 3/2, Pittsburgh, pp. 97-129, https://www.aeaweb.org/articles?id=10.1257/pol.3.2.97.

Hendy, R. (2011), *On Marriage and Labour Market Transitions: A Structural Dynamic Model*, World Bank, Washington, DC, http://siteresources.worldbank.org/EXTABCDE/Resources/7455676-1292528456380/7626791-1303141641402/7878676-1306270833789/Parallel-Session-13-Rana_Hendy.pdf.

Heckman, J. and D. Masterov (2007), "The productivity argument for investing in young children", *NBER Working Paper*, No. 13016, National Bureau of Economic Research, Cambridge, Massachusetts, www.nber.org/papers/w13016.pdf.

Heckman J. et al. (2010), "A new cost-benefit and rate of return analysis for the Perry Preschool Program: A summary", *IZA Policy Papers*, No. 17, IZA, Bonn, http://ftp.iza.org/pp17.pdf.

Hijab, N. (2013), "Regression or progress? Barriers to equality of economic opportunity and the Arab transitions", International Labour Office, Geneva, www.ilo.org/wcmsp5/groups/public/---arabstates/---ro-beirut/documents/genericdocument/wcms_220911.pdf.

ILO (2015), "Women in business and management: Gaining momentum 2015", International Labour Office, Geneva, www.ilo.org/wcmsp5/groups/public/---dgreports/---dcomm/---publ/documents/publication/wcms_316450.pdf.

ILO (2014a), "Global employment trends 2014: Risk of a jobless recovery?", International Labour Office, Geneva, www.ilo.org/wcmsp5/groups/public/---dgreports/---dcomm/---publ/documents/publication/wcms_233953.pdf.

ILO (2014b), "Labour inspection, gender equality and non-discrimination in the Arab states", International Labour Office, Beirut, www.ilo.org/wcmsp5/groups/public/---arabstates/---ro-beirut/documents/publication/wcms_249296.pdf.

ILO (2011), "Database of conditions of work and employment laws", International Labour Office, Geneva, www.ilo.org/dyn/travail.

ILO (2009), "Global employment trends for women: March 2008", International Labour Office, Geneva, www.ilo.org/wcmsp5/groups/public/---dgreports/---dcomm/documents/publication/wcms_091225.pdf.

ILO (2007), "ABC of women workers' rights and gender equality", International Labour Office, Geneva, www.ilo.org/wcmsp5/groups/public/---dgreports/---gender/documents/publication/wcms_087314.pdf.

ILO (2006), "Global employment trends for youth", International Labour Office, Geneva, www.ilo.org/wcmsp5/groups/public/---dgreports/---dcomm/documents/publication/wcms_077664.pdf.

ILO (1996), "Equality in employment and occupation", International Labour Conference, 83rd session, Geneva, www.ilo.org/public/libdoc/ilo/P/09661/09661%281996-83-4B%29.pdf.

ILO (1988), "Equality in employment and occupation: General survey by the committee of experts on the application of conventions and recommendations", International Labour Conference, 75th Session, www.ilo.org/public/libdoc/ilo/P/09661/09661%281988-75-4B%29.pdf.

IMF (2013), "Arab Policy Forum on Financial Inclusion: Addressing challenges of financial inclusion in the Arab world", a speech by Masood Ahmed, www.imf.org/external/np/speeches/2013/121013.htm.

Johansson, E. (2010), "The effect of own and spousal parental leave on earnings", Working Paper 2010, No. 4, Institute for Labour Market Policy Evaluation, Uppsala, Sweden, https://www.econstor.eu/bitstream/10419/45782/1/623752174.pdf.

Lohmann, T. (2010), "Labor regulation and female labor market participation: A country study of Egypt", Economic Integration of Women-MENA, Deutsche Gesellschaft für Technische Zusammenarbeit (GTZ) GmbH, Bonn, http://econowin.org/wp-content/uploads/2014/11/Labor-Regulation-and-Female-Labor-Market-Participation-in-Egypt.pdf.

Ludwig, J. and D. Miller (2007), "Does Head Start improve children's life chances? Evidence from a regression discontinuity design", *Quarterly Journal of Economics*, Vol. 122/1, Chicago, pp. 159-208, http://home.uchicago.edu/~ludwigj/papers/QJE_Headstart_2007.pdf.

McLindon, M. et al. (1999), "Enhancing Egypt's social insurance system", TAPR Project, US AID, Office of Economic Growth, Sector Policy Division, Cairo, http://pdf.usaid.gov/pdf_docs/Pnacx989.pdf.

Milieu Ltd. (2011), "Comparative study on access to justice in gender equality and anti-discrimination law", Synthesis report, DG Justice of the European Commission, Brussels, http://ec.europa.eu/justice/gender-equality/files/conference_sept_2011/final_report_access_to_justice_final_en.pdf.

Ministère des Finances d'Algérie (2013), "Enquête nationale sur l'emploi du temps en Algérie ENET 2012", Rapport d'enquête, Office National des Statistiques, Algiers, www.ons.dz/IMG/pdf/RAPPORT_ENET_2012_FRAN_2_.pdf.

Mryyan, N. (2012), "Demographics, labor force participation and unemployment", ERF Working Paper, No. 670, Economic Research Forum, Cairo, http://erf.org.eg/wp-content/uploads/2014/08/670.pdf.

National Institute for Child Health and Human Development (2003), "Does amount of time in child care predict socio-emotional adjustment during the transition to kindergarten?", *Child Development*, Vol. 74, pp. 976-1005, http://onlinelibrary.wiley.com/doi/10.1111/1467-8624.00582/abstract.

National Institute for Child Health and Human Development (2001), "Nonmaternal care and family factors in early development: An overview of the NICHD study of early child care", *Journal of Applied Developmental Psychology*, Vol. 22, pp. 457-92, http://dx.doi.org/10.1016/S0193-3973(01)00092-2.

Ñopo, H., N. Daza and J. Ramos (2011), "Gender earnings gaps in the world", *IZA Discussion Paper*, No. 5736, IZA, Bonn, http://ssrn.com/abstract=1855188.

Nordman, C. and F. Wolff (2006), "Is there a glass ceiling in Morocco? Evidence from matched worker-firm data", *Journal of African Economies*, Vol. 18/4, pp. 592-633, http://citeseerx.ist.psu.edu/viewdoc/download?doi=10.1.1.190.2745&rep=rep1&type=pdf.

OECD (2016a), "2015 OECD recommendation of the Council on Gender Equality in Public Life", OECD Publishing, Paris, http://dx.doi.org/10.1787/9789264252820-en.

OECD (2016b), *Dare to Share: Germany's Experience Promoting Equal Partnership in Families*, OECD Publishing, Paris, http://dx.doi.org/10.1787/9789264259157-en.

OECD (2016c), *OECD Family Database*, OECD Publishing, Paris, www.oecd.org/els/family/database.htm.

OECD (2016d), "Who uses childcare? Inequalities in the use of formal early childhood education and care (ECEC) among very young children", Backgrounder document, *OECD Family Database*, www.oecd.org/els/family/database.htm.

OECD (2015a), *G20/OECD Principles of Corporate Governance*, OECD Publishing, Paris, http://dx.doi.org/10.1787/9789264236882-en.

OECD (2015b), *OECD Guidelines on Corporate Governance of State-Owned Enterprises*, 2015 Edition, OECD Publishing, Paris, http://dx.doi.org/10.1787/9789264244160-en.

OECD(2015c), "SIGI regional report: Europe and Central Asia", OECD Publishing, Paris, https://www.oecd.org/dev/development-gender/SIGI-BrochureECA-2015-web.pdf.

OECD (2015d), *Women in Public Life: Gender, Law and Policy in the Middle East and North Africa*, OECD, Paris.

OECD (2014), *Women in Business 2014: Accelerating Entrepreneurship in the Middle East and North Africa Region*, OECD Publishing, Paris, http://dx.doi.org/10.1787/9789264213944-en.

OECD/CAWTAR (2014), *Women in Public Life: Gender, Law and Policy in the Middle East and North Africa*, OECD Publishing, Paris, http://dx.doi.org/10.1787/9789264224636-en.

OECD (2013), *PISA 2012 Results: Excellence Through Equity: Giving Every Student the Chance to Succeed*, OECD Publishing, Paris, http://dx.doi.org/10.1787/9789264201132-en.

OECD (2012), *Closing the Gender Gap: Act Now*, OECD Publishing, Paris, http://dx.doi.org/10.1787/9789264179370-en.

OECD Development Centre (2012), *Social Institutions and Gender Index: Understanding the Drivers of Gender Inequality*, Paris, www.genderindex.org/.

OECD (2011), *Doing Better for Families*, OECD Publishing, Paris, http://dx.doi.org/10.1787/9789264098732-en.

OECD (2009), *Doing Better for Children*, OECD Publishing, Paris, http://dx.doi.org/10.1787/empl_outlook-2010-en.

OECD, "Supporting women as economic actors during the transition period", unpublished reports by Algeria, Egypt, Jordan, Libya, Morocco and Tunisia, www.oecd.org/mena/competitiveness/supporting-women-as-economic-actors.htm.

Peebles, D. et al. (2007), "Factors affecting women's participation in the private sector in Jordan", a report for Al-Manar Project, National Centre for Human Resource Development, Canadian International Development Agency, Amman, Jordan, www.almanar.jo/en/documents/Mayssa%20Gender%20report.pdf.

Pieters, J. (2013), "Youth employment in developing countries", *IZA Research Report*, No. 58, IZA, Bonn, www.iza.org/en/webcontent/publications/reports/report_pdfs/iza_report_58.pdf.

Reich, N. (2010), "Who cares? Determinants of the fathers' use of parental leave in Germany", *HWWI Working Paper*, No. 1-31, Hamburg Institute of International Economics, Hamburg, http://econpapers.repec.org/paper/zbwhwwirp/1-31.htm.

Ruhm, C. and J. Waldfogel (2011), "Long-term effects of early childhood care and education", *IZA Discussion Papers*, No. 6149, IZA, Bonn, http://ftp.iza.org/dp6149.pdf.

Sayre, E. and R. Hendy (2013), "Female labour supply in Egypt, Tunisia and Jordan", https://www.aeaweb.org/aea/2014conference/program/retrieve.php?pdfid=398.

Sieverding, M. and I. Selwaness (2012), "Social protection in Egypt: A policy overview", *Gender and Work in the MENA Region Working Papers*, No. 23, Population Council, Cairo, www.popcouncil.org/uploads/pdfs/wp/mena/23.pdf.

Stampini, M. and A. Verdier-Chouchane (2011), "Labour market dynamics in Tunisia: The issue of youth unemployment", *Review of Middle East Economics and Finance*, Vol. 7/2, pp. 1-35, www.afdb.org/fileadmin/uploads/afdb/Documents/Publications/Working%20Paper%20%20No%20123%20%20PDF%20%20.pdf.

Steer, L., H. Ghanem and M. Jalbout (2014), "Arab youth: Missing educational foundations for a productive life?", Brookings Institution, Washington, DC, https://www.brookings.edu/wp-content/uploads/2014/02/arabworld_learningbarometer_en.pdf.

Stein A. et al. (2013), "The influence of different forms of early childcare on children's emotional and behavioural development at school entry", *Child: Care, Health and Development*, Vol. 39/5, pp. 676-687, http://onlinelibrary.wiley.com/doi/10.1111/j.1365-2214.2012.01421.x/abstract.

Sweidan, M. (2012), "Male-female pay differences, Jordanian case", *NECE Working Paper*, No. 23, Konferenz der europäischen Statistiker, Wirtschaftskommission für Europa, Geneva, www.unece.org/fileadmin/DAM/stats/documents/ece/ces/ge.30/2012/Item_2-_Jordan-_Gender_Pay_Gap_final_version.pdf.

Sylva, K., I. Siraj-Blatchford and B. Taggart (2011), *Assessing Quality in the Early Years*, Teachers College Press, New York.

Thévenon O. (2016), "Do "institutional complementarities' foster female labour force participation?", *Journal of Institutional Economics*, Vol. 12/2, pp. 471-497, http://dx.doi.org/10.1017/S1744137415000399.

Thévenon, O. (2013), "Drivers of female labour force participation in the OECD", *OECD Social, Employment and Migration Working Papers*, No. 145, OECD Publishing, Paris, http://dx.doi.org/10.1787/5k46cvrgnms6-en.

Tijdens, K. and M. Van Klaveren (2012), "Frozen in time: Gender pay gap unchanged for 10 years, ITUC, Brussels, www.ituc-csi.org/frozen-in-time-gender-pay-gap.html.

UNESCO (2012), *Youth and Skills: Putting Education to Work*, UNESCO Publishing, Paris, http://unesdoc.unesco.org/images/0021/002180/218003e.pdf.

UNICEF (2014), "Regional report on out-of-school children", Middle East and North Africa Out-Of-School Children Initiative, UNICEF Middle East and North Africa, Amman, www.uis.unesco.org/Education/Documents/oosci-report-mena.pdf.

UN Women (2011), *Progress of the world's women: In pursuit of justice*, UN Women, New York, www.unwomen.org/~/media/headquarters/attachments/sections/library/publications/2011/progressoftheworldswomen-2011-en.pdf.

van Huizen, Th. and J. Plantenga (2015), "Universal child care and children's outcomes: A meta-analysis of evidence from natural experiments", *USE Discussion Paper Series*, No. 15-13, Utrecht University School of Economics, Utrecht, Netherlands, www.uu.nl/sites/default/files/rebo_use_dp_2015_15-13.pdf.

World Bank (2015), *World Bank Entrepreneurial Statistics 2015* (database), World Bank, Washington, DC, http://data.worldbank.org/.

World Bank (2014), *World Bank Global Financial Inclusion Database 2014*, World Bank, Washington, DC, www.worldbank.org/en/programs/globalfindex.

World Bank (2013), "Opening doors: Gender equality and development in the Middle East and North Africa", World Bank, Washington, DC, http://documents.worldbank.org/curated/en/338381468279877854/Main-report.

World Bank (2010), "Women, business and the law: Measuring legal gender parity for entrepreneurs and workers in 128 economies", World Bank, Washington, DC, http://wbl.worldbank.org/~/media/WBG/WBL/Documents/Reports/2010/Women-Business-Law.pdf?la=en.

World Bank (2009), "The status and progress of Women in the Middle East and North Africa", World Bank, Washington, DC, http://siteresources.worldbank.org/INTMENA/Resources/MENA_Gender_Compendium-2009-1.pdf.

World Bank/International Finance Corporation (2013), "Women, business and the law 2014: Removing restrictions to enhance gender equality", World Bank/International Finance Corporation, Washington, DC, http://wbl.worldbank.org/~/media/WBG/WBL/Documents/Reports/2014/Women-Business-and-the-Law-2014-FullReport.pdf?la=en.

Annex 4.A1

Labour equality in domestic laws

Algeria

The Labour Relations Law of 1990 governs private relations, and the Public Officials Status Law of 2006 governs relations in the public sector.

Article 84 of the 1990 Labour Relations Law: "Employers must ensure equality in remuneration between workers for equal work without discrimination."

Article 17 of the 1990 Labour Relations Law: "Any provision within a collective agreement or convention or employment contract that establishes discrimination of any kind between workers with respect to work, remuneration and working conditions on the basis of age, sex, social or marital status, family relationships, political belief, union membership is null and void."

Article 27 of the 2006 Public Officials Status Law: "There shall be no discrimination between public servants on the basis of their sex."

Egypt

The 2003 Labour Law governs private- and public-sector employees; and employment of public-sector employees is regulated by Laws 47 and 48 of 1978 on public-sector employees.

Article 35 of the 2003 Labour Code: "Discrimination in wages on the basis of different sex, origin, language, religion or creed is prohibited."

Article 88: "Subject to the provisions of the following articles, all provisions regulating the employment of workers shall apply to women workers without discrimination once their working conditions are analogous."

Jordan

Labour law is governed in the private sector by the Labour Law of 1996, as amended in 2002, and in the public sector by the Civil Service Regulation of 2007.

Article 4 of the 2007 Civil Service Regulation: "Civil service is based on the following principles and values: 1. Equal opportunities through non-discrimination on the basis of sex, race, religion or social status (…)".

Libya

The Labour Relations Law of 2010 applies to labour relations in both the private and public sectors.

Article 2 of the 2010 Labour Code: "Work is a right for all citizens in Libya, male and female, based on the principle of equality between them…"

Article 3 of the 2010 Labour Code: "Filling jobs and occupations in all workplaces and production should be based on competence, merit and capability and the choice between the candidates should be conducted on the basis of integrity, transparency and justice and not on favouritism or discrimination because of trade union membership, social origin or any other discriminatory reasons."

Article 21 of the 2010 Labour Code: "Difference in financial compensation for work of equal value, based upon sex, colour, religion or ethnicity, is not allowed."

Morocco

The 2003 Labour Law governs relations between persons bound by an employment contract, and the General Statute of the Public Service adopted in 1958 regulates the rights and duties of civil servants. New regulations have been drafted but not adopted yet.

Article 9.2 of the Labour Code: "Any discrimination among employees based on race, colour, gender, handicap, marital status, religion, political opinion, union affiliation, ethnic origin or social status which violates or infringes the principle of equal opportunity or equal treatment in employment or job occupation, especially in respect of hiring, the performance and distribution of work, occupational training, pay, promotion, benefits, disciplinary actions and dismissal is forbidden."

Article 346 of the Labour Code: "Gender-based wage discrimination for work of equal value is prohibited."

Article 1 of the 1958 General Statute of the Public Service: "All Moroccans are entitled to access under conditions of equality to public employment. Subject to the provisions contained therein or resulting from particular statutes, no distinction shall be made between the sexes in the application of this statute."

Tunisia

The labour code, adopted in 1966 and amended several times thereafter, organises work in the private sector. Work in the public sector is governed by the 1983 Ordinance on Civil Servants concerning general statutes for employees of the state, local government and public administrative bodies.

Article 5 bis of the Labour Code, as amended in 1993: "There shall be no discrimination between men and women in the implementation of the provisions of the present code and the texts adopted for its implementation."

Article 11 of the 1983 Law concerning general statutes for employees of the state, local government and public administrative bodies: "Subject to the special provisions dictated by the nature of the duties to be performed and that may be taken in this regard, no distinction shall be made between men and women in the application of this law."

Annex A

Annex to the acknowledgements

The methodology for elaboration of the country reports that supported this publication was standard across countries. In-depth desk research by local consultants on domestic legal provisions was complemented by national consultations among experts from a wide spectrum of backgrounds (see “Acknowledgements”, above). In addition, focus groups were organised with local stakeholders, including entrepreneurs, undergraduate business students in their final year, unemployed women, women working in remote regions and, where possible, women working from home. These exchanges enriched the research findings with insights from life experiences, and also raised awareness about women’s rights. In Libya, the ongoing conflict affected access to data and limited the possibility of reaching out to focus groups. Focus group participants are listed below, along with colleagues from the OECD who provided input to the publication.

Focus group participants

Algeria

Students’ names were not registered, and the 40 or so entrepreneurs and researchers who commented upon the national research and findings have requested anonymity.

Egypt

Entrepreneurs:

Abir Essawy, Amina Meaad, Azza Abdel Wahab, Carole Cranmer, Dalia El Batal, Dalia Kabeel, Dina Aly, Effat El Shooky, Eman Abdel Hamer, Farida Abdel Latif, Farida Ali, Hala Ahmed Salih, Hanan Hassan Mahmoud, Heba Gamal, Heba Hosni Gamal, Heba Makled, Hoda Kamal, Howaida Korat, Iman El Garhy, Lina Al Khatib, Lisa Heermann, Magy Selwanes, Maha Mahgob, Manal Mahmoud, Marwa Wafik, Mohamed Noweir, Muhammad Mansour, Nadia Khairy, Nagla Sayed Sofy, Naglaa Ali, Nanies Abdel Latif, Nariman Abdel Kader, Rania Habib, Rasha Mohamed Abdel Monem, Rashad Lamada, Riham Abo Elinin, Sahar Nazmy, Salma Magdy el Kazabgy, Soraya Mansour, Susan Kamal, Suzan Hamed, Walid Hamed, Yara Eid and Youmna El Shereidi.

Handicraft women in remote areas: The national team met 10 women in Faioum (Khalta village) and 20 women in Qena.

Students:

Reem El Menshawy, Alia Adel Soliman, Alia Ahmed Fawzy El Sayed, Asmaa Ahmed Youssef, Asmaa Mohamed Ezzat, Aya Essam El Din Abdel Halim, Eman Mahmoud, Engy Abel Wahab, Engy Mohamed Hendai, Farida Khaled Kotb, Fatma Mosaad Abel Ghany, Heinar Hesham, Mai Atef Al-Sayed Abul-Aziz, Mariam Hussein Al-Masry, Mariam Tharwat Zaki Mecky, Maryam Samy Abdel-Ghaffar, Noura Magdi Abdel-Moamen, Nourhan Hossam El Dien Yakout, Rana Ahmed Mohamed, Rana Lotfy and Sarah El-Gerby.

Others:

Amal Amaar, Eman El Kemry, Heba Moghaieb, Isis Hafez, Marwa Soudi, Nariman Abdel Kader Mona Ezzat Sabrine Assem and Shehata Al-Guindi.

Jordan

Youth from Karakand Tafila:

Hamzeh Khaldi, Hamzeh Sarayreh, Mohammad Madadha, Samer Mubeidean, Farah Majali, Hala Khatatneh, Hala Ma'aytah, Majd Rawashdeh, Mayyadah O'roud, Mira Ma'aytah Rawan, Khatatneh and Zara Ma'aytah, Aroub Al Soubh, Ahmad Ra'oud, Amira Shabatat, Hanin Shqareen, Ibrahim Sabayleh, Khaled Ramadan, Lina A'wamreh, Majd Qatameen, Maysoun Tawabeh, Rashed Ra'oud and Sahar Al A'wadat.

Economic and gender experts:

Dr. Ashraf Al Omari, the inspector of Sharia courts.

Ms. Haifa Al Najjar, member of the upper house of parliament and superintendent of the Ahliyyah School for Girls (ASG) and the Bishop's School (BSA) for Boys.

H.E. Ms. Nesreen Barakat, who was minister of social development in 2012, minister of public sector development in 2010 and is currently managing director of Excel Consulting.

Dr. Ibtisam Al Ayoubi, general manager of Qurtoba for Capacity Building and Administrative Solutions and board member of the Jordanian National Forum for Women; Ms. Hala Bsaisu, managing director at AYA Consultancy for Development, former minister of social development and former director of the office of Her Majesty Queen Rania Al Abdullah; and Iman Al Damen, banking consultant and member of the Jordanian National Forum for Women and the Jordan Forum for Business and Professional Women.

Libya (due to security considerations, consultations were limited)

Entrepreneurs:

Bahia Kanoun, Faisel Miloud, Fatma Hgig, Howida Diab, Islam Zriba, Laila Almsrati, Najlaa Ali, Alzarougi, Omnia Tayri, Rida Atubli, Saher Arkano, Turkia Abd Alhfid and Wasef Albadrani.

Morocco

Entrepreneurs:

Afifa Boutaleb, Alami, Dounia Boutaleb, Fatiha Daoudi, Fethia Sefrioui, Laila Miyara, Nadia Jalal, Naima, Ourdane, Nawal Houti, Rajaa Mammou Jallal, Soraya Sebbani, Wassila Kara Ibrahimi, Nawal Houti.

Youth seeking employment:

Asmaa Ettoubali, Debbagh El Mehdi, El Fakrouni Taoufik, Hadil Tarfaoui, Hajar Boumehdi, Ilham ZRIG, Moulabbi Boutaina, Oussama Essafiani and Tahri Chaimae.

Students:

Asmaa Bahreddine, Boutaina Bassim, Dounia Rouqui, Fadoua Farachi, Fatimazahra Bouzidi, Laila Ghachy, Laila Ghachy, Laila Senhaji, Leila Ghorby, Leila Ghorby, Manal Elouraoui, Najwa Jaawani, Sofia Joudat, Soukaina Jaouhari, Sofia Joudat, Soukaina Jaouhari and Yasmine Atouk.

Others:

Abdessamad Sadouk, Abid Kabadi, Ahmed Abbadi, Ahmed Almotamassik, Ahmed Lahlimi Alami, Alaoui Anouar, Driss Alaoui Mdaghri, Hajbouha Zoubeir, Jamal Belahrach, Khadija Riyadi, Khalid Dahami, Manal Elouraoui, Mohamed Chafiki, Mounir Ferram, Nezha Taârji Marrakchi, Oumnia Sbai and Tabit Larbi.

An inter-governmental consultation was organised in May 2015 by Minister Mohamed El Louafa at which all ministries were represented (over 100 participants).

Tunisia

Entrepreneurs:

Abid Khemiri, Amel Hantous, Ben Alaya Sourour, Ben Khelifa Zouhaira, Emmanuel Gélis-Diaz, Hafidha Merdassi, Leila Benkhiria, Loussaief Hanen, Lydie Mouret, Madame Afifa, Ms. Ben Hammouda, Mounira Hamdi, Rafiaa Amdouni, Rim Essaidi and Zakia Souaifi.

Students:

Bouhlel Mohamed, Charfeddine Emna, Chebbi Ameni, Dhif Fairouz, Donia Barakati, Fatma Ktari Gana, Mohamed Anis, Ghaoui Hiba, Haamdi Manel, Hajer BenMessaoud, Ines Trabelsi, Maafi Hiba, Nadia Hela Doudech, Rokbani Rim, Sarra Chaouach, Sebai Leila, Sonia Ben Majed, Tlili Farah, Troudi Yossra and Zaineb Bouaasida.

Women seeking employment:

Ahlem Ayadi, Ayadi Ameni, Ayari Samira Ben Said, Dhoha BenBachir, Hiba Bhiri, Fatma Bhiri, Wafa Chelladi, Monia Donia Zghidi, Essayeh Nadia, Gaidi Yosra, Hamida Ifa, Hannachi Eya, Ines Ben Ali, Jobrani Wassila, Mchergui Imene, Mezni Olfa, Mhidi Hana, Monser Najet, Ochi Sana and Soumaya Haj Hamma.

Government and non-government institutions:

Ahmed Ben Aicha, Aicha Karafi, Anis Khanech, Ayda Ben Chaabane, Eljezia Hammami, Emna Aouadi, Hajer Trabelsi, Houda Chahed, Imen Zouaoui, Imene Houimel, Mounira Hammami, Rachida Jebnoun, Samira Merai, Sana Bouzaouche, Sihem Bouras, Sonia Abassi and Thouraya Ben Haj Hammouda.

Annex B

The Social Institutions and Gender Index (SIGI)

The OECD Development Centre's Social Institutions and Gender Index (SIGI) is a cross-country measure of gender-based discrimination in social institutions across 160 countries. The SIGI looks at laws, practises and attitudes across five socio-economic areas that affect women's lives: discriminatory family code, restricted physical integrity, son bias, restricted resources and assets, and restricted civil liberties. By focusing on discriminatory social institutions, the SIGI aims to expose the underlying drivers of gender inequality that block countries' progress towards achieving equal outcomes for women and men.

Despite increasing levels of education and improved health outcomes for women and girls over the past two decades, the Middle East and North Africa (MENA) remains one of the poorer performers in the 2014 edition of the SIGI. Plural legal systems complicate the application of laws pertaining to women's equitable rights in the family involving parental authority, inheritance and access to and control of economic resources. These are exacerbated by inter-household relations that infringe on women's decision-making power and reinforce the unequal distribution of unpaid care work in the home. Violence against women is also a concern, with two-thirds of countries lacking adequate legislation.

While serious challenges remain, the six countries covered in this report provide positive examples of government measures to support women's and girls' rights. Algeria, Egypt, Jordan, Morocco and Tunisia have introduced legislative quotas to promote women's political representation to promising results. In Algeria, for example, women occupy 32% of parliamentary seats, the highest level in the MENA region. All six countries have established the minimum age for marriage at 18 or higher, and Algeria, Libya and Tunisia see some of the lowest early-marriage prevalence rates in the region (1-3%). The report also highlights the important legal changes these countries have made to secure women's rights in the home and at work since the release of SIGI 2014.

Discriminatory social institutions are very costly for MENA countries beyond their negative effect on outcomes for women and girls. Research using the SIGI 2014 results reveals that gender-based discrimination in social institutions represents a cost of USD 575 billion for the region (Ferrant and Kolev, 2016). However, the findings also point to the positive impact that removing these barriers to gender equality could have for both women and men in the region, potentially increasing average income per capita by 0.6 percentage points. Thus, addressing the obstacles to women's and girls' empowerment holds great promise for unlocking inclusive development that benefits entire societies.

References

OECD Development Centre (2014), *Social Institutions and Gender Index Synthesis Report*, OECD Development Centre, Paris.

Ferrant, G. and A. Kolev (2016), "Does gender discrimination in social institutions matter for long-term growth? Cross country evidence", *OECD Development Centre Working Papers No. 330*, OECD, Paris.

ORGANISATION FOR ECONOMIC CO-OPERATION AND DEVELOPMENT

The OECD is a unique forum where governments work together to address the economic, social and environmental challenges of globalisation. The OECD is also at the forefront of efforts to understand and to help governments respond to new developments and concerns, such as corporate governance, the information economy and the challenges of an ageing population. The Organisation provides a setting where governments can compare policy experiences, seek answers to common problems, identify good practice and work to co-ordinate domestic and international policies.

The OECD member countries are: Australia, Austria, Belgium, Canada, Chile, the Czech Republic, Denmark, Estonia, Finland, France, Germany, Greece, Hungary, Iceland, Ireland, Israel, Italy, Japan, Korea, Latvia, Luxembourg, Mexico, the Netherlands, New Zealand, Norway, Poland, Portugal, the Slovak Republic, Slovenia, Spain, Sweden, Switzerland, Turkey, the United Kingdom and the United States. The European Union takes part in the work of the OECD.

OECD Publishing disseminates widely the results of the Organisation's statistics gathering and research on economic, social and environmental issues, as well as the conventions, guidelines and standards agreed by its members.

OECD PUBLISHING, 2, rue André-Pascal, 75775 PARIS CEDEX 16
(03 2017 08 1 P) ISBN 978-92-64-27931-5 – 2017

www.ingramcontent.com/pod-product-compliance
Ingram Content Group UK Ltd.
Pitfield, Milton Keynes, MK11 3LW, UK
UKHW051504290926
15471UKWH00008B/1406

9 789264 279315